3.99.

zP 4/a7

PENGU

WHY VOTE CONSERVATIVE?

David Willetts was educated at King Edward's School, Birmingham, and at Oxford, where he took a First in P Economics. He served as an official in to 1984, including a spell as Private Secretary to Nigel Lawson. He was then a member of Mrs Thatcher's Downing Street Policy Unit. From 1987 to 1992 he was Director of Studies at the Centre for Policy Studies. In 1992 he was elected the Member of Parliament for Havant in Hampshire. He has served as a Government Whip and as Paymaster General in the Cabinet Office. He has been closely involved in the development of Conservative policy over the past decade, and has written widely on economic and social issues. His book *Modern Conservatism* is also published by Penguin.

Why Vote Conservative?

David Willetts MP

PENGUIN BOOKS

PENGUIN BOOKS

Published by the Penguin Group
Penguin Books Ltd, 27 Wrights Lane, London W8 5TZ, England
Penguin Books USA Inc., 375 Hudson Street, New York, New York 10014, USA
Penguin Books Australia Ltd, Ringwood, Victoria, Australia
Penguin Books Canada Ltd, 10 Alcorn Avenue, Toronto, Ontario, Canada M4V 3B2
Penguin Books (NZ) Ltd, 182–190 Wairau Road, Auckland 10, New Zealand

Penguin Books Ltd, Registered Offices: Harmondsworth, Middlesex, England

First published 1997
10 9 8 7 6 5 4 3 2 1

Set in 10.5/12.5pt Monotype Sabon
Typeset by Rowland Phototypesetting Ltd,
Bury St Edmunds, Suffolk
Printed in England by Clays Ltd, St Ives plc

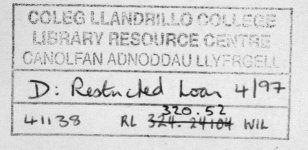

To my parents

Contents

Acknowledgements

I am grateful to Daniel Finkelstein and Rick Nye for their very helpful comments on an earlier draft of this book. I am also grateful to my secretary, Helga Wright, who, as always, has worked with great dedication on this project.

This book draws on previous publications of mine: *Modern Conservatism* (Penguin, 1992); *Civic Conservatism* (Social Market Foundation, 1994); *Blair's Gurus* (Centre for Policy Studies, 1996) and 'The Free Market and Civic Conservatism', which appears in *Conservative Realism: New Essays in Conservatism*, edited by Kenneth Minogue (HarperCollins, 1996).

Finally, I must acknowledge my debt to my fellow MPs. Any Conservative understands that he is working within a tradition far bigger than any one of us. Discussing the issues of the day with friends and colleagues is the best way of exploring that tradition. Without such conversations this book would not have been possible.

Introduction

Some people claim that the two-party battle between Conservative and Labour has become irrelevant. I do not agree with them. T. S. Eliot said of the English Civil War that in a sense it had never ended and Roundheads were still fighting Cavaliers. There is also a fundamental division between the Tory and Labour view of the world. We want to combine the dynamism of the free market with respect for our traditional institutions. Labour, like all radical progressives since the French Revolution, still aim at fundamental transformation achieved by government. I have tried to explain this at greater length elsewhere. This book focuses, however, not on the general truths of Conservatism but the particular reasons why I hope you will vote Conservative in 1997. I hope to persuade you of three things.

First, we can look forward to rising living standards as a result of our success in economic reform. The story of the British economy since the Second World War is not a happy one and recessions hurt. We lagged behind our Continental competitors. But now we can be confident that our economy is better placed to face the challenges of the twenty-first century than the overtaxed, overregulated economies of Continental Europe.

Secondly, these gains would be jeopardized if Tony Blair's Labour Party took office. They want us to copy those very Continental models whose failure is increasingly recognized.

Introduction

His party has indeed changed but New Labour brings new dangers.

The electorate does not cast thank-you votes. They want to know what we offer for the future. The third task is therefore to show the challenges for us to face in our fifth term, and how we intend to spread opportunity for all.

I PRINCIPLES

ONE
The Battle of Ideas

Conservatives have spent this century fighting the battle for personal freedom with energy and with relish. Our opponents, first the New Liberals at the turn of the century, then command-economy socialists, and now Tony Blair's Labour Party, all share a belief in interventionist, intrusive government. Conservatives by contrast trust the people.

Since 1979 Conservative Governments have moved forward like ice-breakers, ploughing their way through the frozen wastes of state control. Back then the state tried to fix the price of goods in the shops. It tried to fix the pay which people received and threatened to blacklist and withhold contracts from firms which did not pay the rates which government thought right. It controlled the amount of money which companies could distribute in dividends to put into our pension funds. It controlled how many pounds we could take abroad. Now all that seems incredible. Anybody who tried to argue for such policies would be laughed out of court. We have won a great victory.

There are several reasons for our victory. One is the sheer intellectual creativity of free-market economics over the past twenty years. Great excitement and energy has been generated by applying elementary economic tools (supply and demand, cost–benefit analysis, the price mechanism), to areas which are wrongly thought to be somehow immune from rational economic appraisal. A rich and ambitious policy agenda has developed – including privatization, tax reform, and internal

1

markets within the public sector. Free marketeers have generated the ideas and ideas matter in politics.

Technology and industrial change have also been on our side, promoting individualism both in production and in consumption. For most of this century the dominant industrial model was large-scale manufacturing, with hundreds of workers carrying out virtually identical tasks on long production lines. Now large firms are a declining proportion of total national output and employment. We see the rise of small firms and larger enterprises restructuring so that people work in smaller groups. Rewards are increasingly not fixed on some standardized basis but individually determined (and our left-wing egalitarians, so preoccupied with explaining greater dispersion of income in terms of the tax and benefits system, completely fail to understand that the crucial explanation is greater tailoring of pay to personal skills). Technology also makes market solutions practical in areas where they were just theoretical curiosities in the past.

Internationally there was a Manichaean battle between the West and an 'evil empire'. The Soviet Union was not just a hostile power as normally understood by diplomats; it was also, as Burke called the French Revolution, an 'armed doctrine'. The collapse of the empire finally revealed the bankruptcy of the doctrine. Market capitalism is now once more the model to which almost the entire world aspires.

Above all, the appeal to personal freedom has a moral authority which it is almost impossible to challenge. As Margaret Thatcher so powerfully showed, people respond to the message that they are free to choose, can seize opportunities, can make their own way in the world and can take responsibility for the consequences of their own actions.

The power of free-market thinking, the drive of technology, the collapse of Marxism, the moral authority of the appeal to personal freedom, all mean that modern Conservatives ought to feel that the tide of ideas and events is in our favour. The main problem facing Conservatism in Britain should be triumphalism and complacency. That vigorous, exhilarating battle over the past twenty years should have left us enjoying the same domination of the political scene as Liberalism enjoyed in the middle of the last century.

By and large, parties which win the battle of ideas so comprehensively stay in office for a generation. It is wrong to think of British policies as somehow delivering frequent and regular changes of government. In practice in Britain, as in many other advanced Western countries, the tendency has been for a dominant party to emerge which captures the spirit of the age and carries it forward. Modern Conservatives occupy precisely such a position in Britain today.

On some measures that dominance is clear – nearly eighteen years in government is no mean feat. But in other ways Conservatives can still feel like an embattled minority: the media, the Church, academia, are still largely uncomprehending and the conventional wisdom hostile. Despite all the advances we have made since 1979, the collapse of the socialist Left has not given Conservatives the intellectual dominance which we deserve.

Our victory has felt strangely qualified and partial because there are still many people in this country who are uncomfortable with the free market. The Labour Party speaks for them. Their language may have shifted from Fabian socialism to stakeholding and social cohesion but they are still exploiting misconceptions and misunderstandings about the free market. So we must start, in these first three chapters, by trying to clear these away and showing how now the free market ties in to modern Conservatism. Then we can turn to the big practical issues.

Middle England

The Conservative Party has been in office on its own or with others for most of this century. This is not a series of flukes or the result of extraordinarily ingenious manipulations of the economy. It is because the Conservative Party is the party of Middle England (and Wales and Scotland). We are deeply rooted in the institutions and ways of life which make our country what it is. That is why people who are non-political are Conservatives. It is what our opponents with their radical ideas for transforming our country most dislike about us. Today's most influential and widely quoted radical thinker, Will Hutton, rightly recognizes in his book, *The State We're In*, that the main threat to his agenda is the Conservative Party, which he describes as 'finding Middle England's centre of gravity and ensuring that no other party endangers Middle England's pleasures and privileges'.

It is not as if the Conservative Party cynically sets about trying to work out what Middle England wishes and then delivers it. The Conservative Party *is* Middle England: you do not need a focus group to find out what your own family thinks. And what is it that the typical British citizen wants? Underneath the shifting debates on particular issues one can identify two central aspirations. First, we want freedom and opportunity – to feel that we can make life better for ourselves and our families. The most practical expression of this is that we hope to enjoy a rising standard of living. We expect cars to improve, shops to get brighter, magazines to become livelier, hi-fi to continue to get cheaper, our choice of holidays to become wider. We want to feel that as consumers we are sovereign and that if the goods or services we buy are shoddy then we can take our custom elsewhere. This is the power of the consumer in a modern free-market economy: free, mobile, individualistic. Such a society is based on contract not status. It is innovative, striving, enterprising.

We want something else too – to know who we are, bound by ties of affinity. We want to feel that we have roots and are not just leading a life which is a series of meaningless acts of consumption strung together. We want to be linked to the past through traditions and institutions that are far bigger than any individual. We want to live in a society where people matter to each other, not because we are Mother Theresas giving up everything to care for other people, but because experiences which are shared are often more real and more satisfying. We do not want to share our property in pursuit of some egalitarian vision but we do want to feel that we are part of one nation where the successes and the travails of the Royal family or sportsmen and women or indeed the stars of the popular soaps, give us something which we share with others and can talk about with them. We want a society where there are thick social ties, and lumpy local loyalties, not one which has been finely graded into individual grains moving frictionlessly past each other. We want a society of history and traditions, cohesiveness and community – what John Major has called 'a nation at ease with itself'.

Each one of us in our own lives is trying to balance these two conflicting pressures. Do you move house to get a better job if it means leaving your friends and disrupting your child's education? Do you drive to the out-of-town superstore or do you pay a bit more at the local shop? Do you split up from your partner when you are not getting on or do you think it is a long-term relationship you should stick to through a rough patch?

These are not just personal questions: they are at the heart of much political theory. It is the tension between 'Gesellschaft' – the anonymous structure of transactions and rules in a modern free-market society – and 'Gemeinschaft' – the close ties of community where understandings do not have to be explicit because they are so deeply shared.

These two principles can both be traced far back in the tradition of Conservative thought. The excitement and dynamism of Conservatism this century has been generated by a creative tension between these two principles: our belief on the one hand in individual freedom, private property, and the market economy; and on the other hand a commitment to maintaining the institutions which hold our nation together. After the Second World War and the Labour landslide of 1945 the young Tory thinkers of the One Nation group such as Enoch Powell and Iain Macleod reconciled these two principles in the following way:

To a Tory the nation is not primarily an economic entity. It may place political and social ends above purely economic ones, and for their sake may justifiably on occasion seek to prevent change or divert it. Yet economic change is the normal environment in which nations live, and successful adjustment to it is a condition of their well-being. In six years of war and six of Socialism this important truth was dangerously obscured and overlaid. We doubt if it yet claims sufficient attention.

Conservatives understand that government should stay out of the way as far as possible so that economic change is not obstructed. But when it comes to the constitution or education or crime, then the Conservative Party is the party of order and stability. Our disagreement with Tony Blair's 'New Labour' is that they get this exactly the wrong way round. Labour still want to intervene to stop the processes of economic change, but at the same time they have a restless urge to change our ways of governing ourselves. It is the party of economic stagnation and restless constitutional innovation. That is not true to Britain and its history.

It would be a failure of imagination for a political party to say to the British people that they could only have half of what they want – either the fruits of economic success or the rootedness of a long-established society (which we will look at in turn in the next two chapters). The party which wins the next election will be the party which can show most persuasively to the British people that it understands how these two desires, each deep-seated and legitimate, can be reconciled. I believe that the only coherent way to reconcile both is to be found in the British Conservative tradition.

TWO

The Free Market

The Free Market: Four Fallacies and a Paradox

The free market is the most dynamic, inventive and liberating economic principle known to man. It is now triumphant across the world. They are privatizing in Peru, cutting taxes in Poland, deregulating in Namibia. It was Ronald Reagan and Margaret Thatcher who showed the way: their influence will be felt around the world for decades to come.

The free market is still widely suspected, even here where it was first systematically explained by Adam Smith in *The Wealth of Nations* in 1776. One sometimes fears we have not got past the intellectual atmosphere pithily described by Walter Bagehot a hundred years later. He said that the doctrine of free trade was indeed 'in the air' but 'it was a tenet against which a respectable parent would probably caution his son – still it was known as a tempting heresy against which a warning was needed'. Labour try to exploit these doubts with a soft language of stakeholding and social cohesion. So we need to clear away some misconceptions before we move on.

First is the fallacy that 'free markets just mean every man for himself and the devil take the hindmost'. That is not just the view of the average left-wing intellectual. It is also the view of the worldly-wise golf club bore who patronizingly tells the young man that everyone his age ought to be a socialist but when he grows older he will sadly discover that it is a tough world and ultimately we are all in it for ourselves. But economics

7

is not psychology: it is not a theory of human motivation. The motives which drive the entrepreneur are as varied as human nature. He may be trying to make a fortune so as to endow a trust to rescue iguanas or his local football club. The free marketeer is not committed to believing that the only thing which motivates the Wimbledon tennis player is the prize money. All that free-market economics says is that the best tennis comes from matches where the competitors are trying to win.

The second fallacy is that 'you are poor because someone else is rich'. A couple of false assumptions underlie this fallacy. One is the belief that economic relationships take the form of one person exploiting another, whereas every schoolboy knows that if I exchange my old pop record for your poster we can both be better off. We can both gain from trade. Enjoying prosperity is not like being top of the class – a position we can only gain at the expense of someone else. It is instead like being well educated, we can all enjoy it together. The other assumption is that we live in a zero-sum society with only a fixed amount of goods to go around. This is only true in the very short term – it ignores the ability of capitalism to generate growth, even with limited natural resources, by finding new and better ways of doing things. Capitalism is open and dynamic, not closed and static.

Third, there is the fallacy that 'there is no real competition in big-business capitalism'. This misconception can be traced back to the traditional economics textbook which spends the first few chapters setting out an extraordinarily rigorous definition of perfect competition in which every firm simply has to sell its goods at the going price. The rest of the economics course then consists of evidence that markets fail to live up to these special conditions and so if there is any competition at all it is at best imperfect.

This view was then popularized by J. K. Galbraith, probably the most overrated post-war economist. He saw the modern corporation as a big bureaucracy undisturbed by risk or competition because of the power it exerted over its consumers captured by advertising. But try telling that to the management of Texaco or Dunlop or Pan-Am or British Leyland, once proud companies brought low because they failed to keep up with the competition. The competition faced by big corporations is in many ways more real and intense than that faced by small farmers, who can sell however much barley they produce at the going price.

Fourth is the fallacy that 'free markets are immoral because everything has its price'. Egalitarian socialists criticize capitalism on essentially materialistic grounds that it should deliver more creature comforts to the poor. But at the same time the Utopian socialists criticize it on the opposite anti-materialistic grounds – that nothing is sacred in the market-place: it is just a world of things and prices.

It is true that economics is an imperialistic discipline which claims to be able to apply economic calculation to everything – indeed some of the most fruitful advances in the past decade have come from applying economics to new areas such as the law, health care or the family. When cost–benefit analysis is applied to a public-policy problem a price is indeed put on everything – including human life itself. How much should we spend on improving that road to reduce by one the likely number of fatal accidents in the next decade? How much should we spend on a drug that will bring someone another year of life? Some people find the very thought of such questions offensive, because a life is of infinite value, but in a world of limited resources it is right to find the best way of using them. If we spent £10 million on a road bypass to save one life, when the same sum could have been spent on buying a drug to save a thousand lives in the NHS, we have been immoral, not moral. The economic way of thinking is the best way of approaching a problem where resources are limited and have to be put to best use.

Apart from these four fallacies, there is a paradox about the free market too. The crucial insight of free-market economics is that consumers should be sovereign over producers. Adam

Smith robustly stated that 'consumption is the sole end and purpose of production'. That is the clue to the success of a modern market economy: it is an economic democracy in which we all vote with our money. Yet production somehow feels more morally elevated than consumption. We feel we are doing something useful and significant if we teach children, help assemble a motor car, produce a TV series, or work as a hairdresser. People are getting something that they want or need as a result of our efforts. But we are unlikely to feel that it is quite so worthwhile to go shopping, to browse through the TV channels until you find a programme you want to watch, or to spend the morning at the hairdresser's. Production feels more valuable than consumption. Moreover, our interests as consumers are varied but our interests as producers are more narrowly focused and so more vivid.

It is therefore a tempting mistake to look at an economic system from the producer's perspective, not the consumer's. Many businessmen believe that we would be richer if only the Japanese were not so good at making cars and hi-fi equipment. But while the Japanese might make life difficult for our producers, they enrich us all as consumers. We are better off if a Japanese manufacturer makes a more reliable and cheaper car than anyone has before.

There is a final twist to the paradox. We are not just better off as consumers if we are free to choose. Ultimately it is in the best interests of producers too. In a consumer-driven market economy, producers perform to their best and can expand and thrive. It is not in the long-term interests of producers to be protected from the pressures of international competition. The evidence confirms that companies which improve their performance most are those facing the toughest competition.

Enterprise versus Stakeholding

How do these arguments about the free market tie in with the choice facing us at the next general election? Has the Labour

Party now changed so much that all those arguments in favour of the free market which were so controversial even ten years ago have now become part of the common ground of British politics?

The collapse of command-economy socialism has certainly ended the harsh ideological battle between Marxism and capitalism. But we are still told there is an alternative to all this hard-headed free-market economics. Labour believe that the future lies with those Continental social democracies that they praise so frequently. They speak of 'stakeholding' and the 'social partners'. Such beliefs permeate much of the European Commission, and underpin the Social Chapter: it is one reason for Labour's warmth for European federalism.

There is a big choice between on the one hand a free-market economy and on the other hand a stakeholder economy with 'social cohesion' delivered by more regulations and taxation. In a market economy consumers have power over producers whereas in a corporatist economy, producers have power over consumers. It is still a very good test to use when you listen to a politician talking about the economy – whether he or she is approaching it from the point of view of the consumer or the producer.

The Labour Party's gut dislike of the free market is shown in the way they caricature what they call 'Anglo-American capitalism'. They claim, for example, that as free marketeers we believe the response to international competition must be to try to drive pay rates down to levels somewhere between those of Slovakia and Thailand, while pursuing a social policy which is a cross between Hong Kong in 1950 and the London of Charles Dickens.

Their miserable picture of what free markets mean in practice is not borne out by the evidence. Using OECD data, one can compare the annual take-home pay of production workers in various European Union countries at purchasing-parity exchange rates and after direct taxation. For someone who has a family with two children their take-home pay after tax in the

UK in 1994 was £12,000 compared with £12,800 in Germany and £9,800 in France. We are not badly off. But in Britain it still costs less to employ someone than in a number of European countries because we do not have the extra costs of higher taxes and social security contributions added on the Continent. For every £100 paid in wages by employers, there are additional non-wage labour costs of £44 in Italy, £41 in France, £34 in Spain, £32 in Germany, but only £18 in the UK. That is as clear a measure as one could want of the difference between our policies and the high costs of the Continental model so admired by Labour.

Another Labour attack on the free market is that it is 'short-termist' and does not invest enough. That is why they want government to intervene supposedly to strengthen our industrial base. But business investment in Britain has been higher as a share of national income in the 1990s than in the 1980s when it was in turn higher than in the 1970s. The share of our national income which businesses invest is very similar to that of most other advanced economies, but our demanding capital markets mean that the quality of that investment is unusually good. We get more out of every pound invested.

The evidence does not support the belief that the City is only interested in short-term profits. A share price already embodies all known information about a firm and its economic prospects, and so it does indeed tend to react rapidly and dramatically to new information: that is the working of an efficient market. It is not short-termism; indeed, it may react to new information in a dramatic but 'long-term' way. The evidence is that if a company announces a big increase in its R&D expenditure, its share price tends to rise rather than to fall.

What about Japan? Isn't that an example of an industrial strategy working and a clear refutation of the classic free-market model? But there is much mythology about Japan, as Professor Porter of Harvard University explains in his magisterial survey, *The Competitive Advantage of Nations*:

Many Americans think Japanese companies have succeeded because of cooperation, cartels, and government intervention. Japan does have many cartels – such as in agriculture, chemicals, construction, paper and metals – but these are in sectors where Japan is not competitive. In the world-class Japanese industries there are numerous Japanese rivals that have diverse strategies. These companies slug it out daily in the home market. Market shares fluctuate rapidly, as new products and production improvements are introduced at a stunning rate. The lesson to be learned from Japan is that competition works, not that we should limit it.

The best way to improve the performance of British industry is to expose it to as much competition as possible – domestic and international.

The Labour Party's hostility to the modern enterprise economy is expressed in their language of 'stakeholding'. It starts with a proposition that is uncontroversial, even banal. A company's profitability depends on its relationships with a variety of groups – 'stakeholders' if you wish – consumers, investors, workers, and suppliers, etc. But the stakeholder agenda goes further than this: it claims there need to be changes in the way companies are run and that all these different groups should be legally represented on the body which governs the company. This is where we move from platitude to threat.

There is no reason why the interests of these groups should all coincide, certainly not in the short term. Indeed, they may be interests of a fundamentally different type – a supplier's interest in continuing to have a remunerative contract is different from a consumer's interest which may be in a cheaper, more innovative product. The stakeholder agenda does not explain how these different claims are to be balanced. Indeed Labour and the TUC have made it clear that what they mean by the stakeholder talk is old-fashioned, organized trade unions. It would not be possible to preserve the industrial relations success of the past fifteen years if we shifted towards giving trade unions representation on the board.

Many firms proudly regard themselves as stakeholder companies. It has become part of their corporate culture. If it makes sense for them, then so be it. The language of the stakeholder has become almost a cliché in corporate strategy. But it moves from a cliché into a dangerous piece of industrial interventionism if it is transposed from the free decision of an individual company shaping its own character to an attempt by government to interfere with the management of all companies. Individual companies can develop their own styles of management but there is no need for the Government to step in and push for a new uniform pattern of corporate behaviour. It is a great strength of the British business scene that we have Lord Hanson and Anita Roddick, BP and JCB. A more prescriptive pattern of corporate law that tried to oblige them all to run their affairs in the same way would be a threat to British firms' ability to change and experiment.

There is one final point which must surely be conclusive. Setting aside all the elaborate arguments, where do businesses actually move to? Where does a businessman in Osaka or Chicago choose to site his European factory? The evidence is overwhelming. We have attracted 40 per cent of American and Japanese investment in Europe. Our stock of inward investment has gone up from £52 billion in 1986 to £153 billion in 1996. OECD figures show we are second only to the USA as a destination for international direct investment. Of the *Fortune* top one hundred companies in the world, ninety-nine have chosen to locate some of their operations in Britain. Our free-market economy is the one the world's industrialists prefer.

THREE

Is There Such a Thing as Society?

Yes.

You may think Margaret Thatcher gave the game away with
that famous remark of hers but let's look at it in full:

> I think we've been through a period where too many people have been
> given to understand that if they have a problem, it's the government's
> job to cope with it. 'I have a problem, I'll get a grant.' 'I'm homeless,
> the government must house me.' They're casting their problem on
> society. And, you know, there is no such thing as society. There are
> individual men and women, and there are families. And no government
> can do anything except through people, and people must look to
> themselves first. It's our duty to look after ourselves and them, also, to
> look after our neighbour. People have got the entitlements too much
> in mind, without the obligations. There's no such thing as entitlement,
> unless someone has first met an obligation.

That shows a strong sense of duty to others, but doubt about
the state as the vehicle for discharging such obligations. The
critics who dominate the Labour Party and the drawing-rooms
of Islington claim it is not the state but the free market that
destroys social cohesion. Tony Blair himself waxes eloquent
on the subject.

Constant revolutionising of production, uninterrupted disturbance of
all social conditions, everlasting uncertainty and agitation distinguish
the bourgeois epoch from all earlier ones. All fixed, fast-frozen relations,
with their train of ancient and venerable prejudices and opinions are

swept away, all new-formed ones become antiquated before they can ossify. All that is solid melts into air, all that is holy is profaned . . .

Actually that was Karl Marx in the Communist Manifesto of 1848 but New Labour argues in much the same way.

We Conservatives may think of ourselves as ice-breakers but the critics claim we are a demolition squad. When faced with this challenge, the Conservative response over the past twenty years has been to say that a free-market economy generates the resources to pay for the welfare state so we can only 'care' if we are first efficient. (It is, for example, one of the iron laws of post-war government that spending on the National Health Service always rises as a proportion of national income under the Conservatives and falls under Labour. John Major has personally pledged that real spending on the NHS will rise, year on year, throughout our fifth term.) Expenditure on the welfare state is more secure under Conservatives because under Labour Governments it lurches from unsustainable spending sprees to financial crises and emergency cuts.

We must not concede too much ground to our opponents, however. It is wrong to assume that any sort of 'solidarity' with our fellow citizens must be expressed through state activity. In fact big government contributes to the atrophy of a far richer and more satisfying network of non-state activities. That is why Conservatives have always valued the active citizen, civil society, neighbourhood, what the sociologists call the 'mediating structures', and Burke called the 'little platoons'. James Baker, when he was US Secretary of State, visited Romania shortly after the collapse of the Iron Curtain. They explained to him what a serious problem they had looking after their orphans. He said that perhaps volunteers and charities could help. His Romanian interpreter did not understand the concept and eventually asked, 'Do you mean nuns?' That story tells us something important about the difference between free-market Texas and socialist Romania.

The pernicious error, upheld by so many of our *bien pensants* and pundits, is to regard the market as the threat to the rich life of a civil society and the state as somehow embodying or protecting those values. Throughout the post-war period public debate in this country has been preoccupied with the supposed threat to traditional British values from brash market forces while the real threat was coming from the intrusive state. It is as if, like the guns of Singapore, we are armed against the wrong enemy, ready to repel an assault from the forces of vulgar American capitalism, while our society has really been under threat from the enormous powers of our own state. The real tragedy of twentieth-century Britain has been the way in which the state has taken over and then drained the lifeblood from the series of institutions which stood between the individual and the government. Gradually we have lost sight of the virtues of those institutions which thicken our social structure and give it a richness which is lost if it is just individuals facing a Fabian, centralized welfare state. Britain has been, if you like, 'deconstructed'.

We have seen great and proud institutions such as our voluntary hospitals and ancient grammar schools brought under state control. Other institutions like our universities have become so dependent on public funds that they have fallen prey to the disease of believing that the best way to embarrass politicians into giving them more taxpayers' money is to say how terrible things are. The behaviour of too many public-sector bodies and their associated pressure groups reminds one of those nature programmes showing fledglings in a nest with beaks permanently open to attract the harassed parent. And as resources are inevitably finite, the battle is really to attract attention away from their rival siblings – a stark truth which is ignored in polite society. Once an institution has descended to this level, it has indeed come to resemble a dependent infant and should not be surprised if it loses authority and respect.

The critics accuse us of being the centralizers and claim somehow grant-maintained schools and self-governing hospitals are examples of this. But they are actually attempts to give greater power to local institutions within the constraints of public finance. There is a problem of centralization in this country, but it is caused by the intense pressure for equality in the financing and delivery of public services, which brings in the national exchequer as the agent for redistributing resources between different parts of the country. De Tocqueville put the point very neatly:

The foremost or indeed the sole condition required in order to succeed in centralizing the supreme power in a democratic community is to love equality or to get men to believe you love it. Thus, the science of despotism, which was once so complex, has been simplified and reduced, as it were, to a single principle.

Civic Conservatism

Those fears about the destructive forces unloosed by free markets seem absurd and hysterical as soon as one considers people's everyday lives. The experience of working in a large firm whose ultimate objective is to maximize profits is not one of being on your own, in ruthless pursuit of the profit motive. You are working in a team. Sophisticated capitalism is a highly cooperative experience. We have been so preoccupied with looking at competition between different firms that we have largely overlooked the experience of cooperation within the firm.

The British suburb is not a place of rootless, miserable apathy either. People, admittedly, do pursue their material aspirations – to own their house, to be able to afford a good holiday – but these are not immoral or shameful. And at the same time the suburbs comprise rich networks of voluntary associations, from the Rotary Club to the British Legion, from the rota for driving the children to school to the firm's social club. Even that urge to home ownership, satisfied more successfully in the 1980s than in any other decade, has given people new and stronger ties to their neighbourhood. Ownership and belonging go together.

Our civic culture is under greatest strain not in the suburbs but in the inner cities from where so many businesses have fled. It is the absence of a modern capitalist economy which brings the real problems, not its success.

The nineteenth century saw economic and social change just as profound as today. We thrived as a market economy and at the same time as a rich civil society, as Macaulay teasingly observed:

This is the age of societies. There is scarcely one Englishman in ten who has not belonged to some association for distributing books, or for prosecuting them; for sending invalids to the hospital, or beggars to the treadmill, for giving plate to the rich, or blankets to the poor.

Government was limited, but at the same time the Victorians were extraordinarily successful at 'remoralizing' the poor. Rates of crime, drunkenness and illegitimacy, all declined. It is this century which has seen big government elbowing aside working-class self-help and private provision and weakened the institutions which shape our characters.

These arguments are not just matters of political theory. They are paralleled in the popular clichés attacking Conservatism: 'They don't care . . . They would privatize everything if they could . . . It's just me, here and now . . . It's every man for himself . . . Conservatives are only interested in what makes a profit, what pays.' And then Conservatives are told increasingly that we are also bossy, using central government to control us with evermore detailed regulation. This unattractive mixture of rampant individualism and intrusive government is what the hostile commentators wrongly think of as modern Conservatism.

A Conservative understands that, in Quintin Hogg's neat expression, economic liberalism is 'very nearly true'. It is right about the economy, but on its own it will not do as a complete political philosophy. Economic liberals have fought an admirable and successful battle for our interests as consumers to be given priority over our interests as producers as we saw in the previous chapter. But that then leaves the question of who these consumers are; what constrains their immediate appetites; what they are loyal to; what duties they believe they have. The market system is constrained and limited by other values: that is why you cannot sell your children or your vote. Understanding our position in historic communities is essential to answer these deeper questions. The Conservative understands the importance of the instincts and institutions which sustain and shape capitalism.

The truth is that the Conservative stands between the two errors of socialist collectivism and libertarian individualism and, indeed, recognizes that they are mutually dependent. Big government undermines community and leaves us just as atomized individuals expecting the welfare state to do everything. Rampant individualism without ties of duty, loyalty and affiliation is only checked by powerful and intrusive government.

The starting-point for any authentically Conservative approach has to be that Britain is not a lumpy enough country. The progressive agenda for the public sector throughout most of this century has been to eliminate diversity, which was always seen as indefensible discrepancy. Reformers have seen themselves as energetic pastry cooks, wielding a rolling-pin to smooth out the lumps in the dough. They have ended up producing a state which is smoother, more fine ground, than any other in the advanced Western world. Labour still believe in a planning and control model for the public sector. A central part of the Conservative agenda for the fifth term is to push forward that process of shifting power and responsibility back to hospitals, schools, GP practices – local institutions that matter to people.

II POLICIES

FOUR

The Economy: Prosperity or Stagnation

Tackling the British Disease

Back in 1979 we suffered from what the world had come to call the 'British disease'. Since 1870, our output per head had increased less than fourfold whereas the increase averaged more than sixfold in fifteen other major countries. The British disease had two crucial components. First, successive governments failed to set the right financial framework for low inflation. Secondly, the private sector failed to match the performance of our foreign competitors because it was afflicted by increasing burdens of tax and regulation. These two problems reinforced each other. Governments were printing too much money and our weak industrial base meant that money was chasing too few goods. We needed less inflation and more real output. Nigel Lawson set out our new approach to steering the economy:

The conventional post-war wisdom was that unemployment was a consequence of inadequate economic growth and economic growth was to be secured by *macro*-economic policy – the fiscal stimulus of an enlarged budget deficit, with monetary policy (to the extent that it could be said to exist at all) on the whole passively following fiscal policy. Inflation, by contrast, was increasingly seen as a matter to be dealt with by *micro*-economic policy – the panoply of controls and subsidies associated with the era of incomes policy.

But the proper role of each is precisely the opposite of that assigned to it by the conventional post-war wisdom. It is the conquest of inflation, and not the pursuit of growth and employment, which is or should

21

be the objective of macro-economic policy. And it is the creation of conditions conducive to growth and employment, and not the suppression of price rises, which is or should be the objective of micro-economic policy. (Mais Lecture, 18 June 1984)

That summarizes the thinking of all Conservative Chancellors since 1979. We have stuck to it through thick and thin. But has it worked? Let's see what success we have had in dealing with the British disease.

When we came to office in 1979 the crucial test facing the Government was to bring down inflation. The trend was deteriorating. From 1964 to 1970 it had averaged 4·4 per cent, then 9.6 per cent from 1970 to 1974 and 15.8 per cent under the last Labour Government from 1974 to 1979. We have reversed that trend. Since 1979 inflation has averaged 6.1 per cent. Indeed, since the last election we have enjoyed a performance better than any since the Second World War and it has averaged only 2.8 per cent. The Government aims to reduce underlying inflation to the lower half of the 1–4 per cent target range and to keep it at 2.5 per cent or less thereafter.

No one believed us when we said back in 1979 that we would crack this central problem, which had defeated successive British governments – but we did it. And we have delivered it by sticking to the basic tenets of monetarism so mocked by the *bien pensants*, who preferred prices and incomes policies fixed by the social partners. To keep inflation down requires skill and determination: now we have shown we can deliver, it is too easily taken for granted. The Labour Party would undermine the credibility of our inflation target by introducing a separate growth target – as Harold Wilson tried in the 1960s. It is like a reformed alcoholic deciding to try just a drop again: it is the road to disaster.

The other half of the British disease was the weakness of our industry – the supply side of the economy. We also have an agenda for dealing with that. We started first by tackling the worst single problem affecting British industry –

catastrophically bad industrial relations. It is not new for Labour 'modernizers' to try to claim they can handle the unions – Harold Wilson tried in the 1960s – but they could not deliver because their own stakeholding policies give unions a bigger role.

The very first act of the Labour Party after it was created in 1906, indeed the main reason for its creation, was to get the newly elected Liberal Government to pass a law – the 1906 Trades Disputes Act – giving trade unions special legal immunity from claims for compensation for damages they caused a person or a business in pursuit of an industrial dispute. Our approach since 1979 has been to cut back these immunities, restricting them to official disputes after a secret postal ballot and outlawing secondary action against others not directly involved. We have increased the rights of individual working men and women (who do not have to join a closed shop now, for example) and of individual trade unionists (who have to be balloted before a strike) at the expense of the old trade-union bosses. We now propose further improvements within this framework of law to remove immunities where strikes do disproportionate damage to the public.

We can see the benefits of our reforms if we take a step back and look at the overall trend. During the 1970s on average 12.9 million working days were lost through strikes per year. In the 1980s that was down to an average of 7.2 million per year. During the 1990s it has fallen to an average of 0.75 million per year. The remaining problem – as we have recently seen – is concentrated almost entirely in the few remaining bits of the old industrial public sector.

The chairman of BMW, Bernd Pischetsrieder, has summarized our achievements very clearly:

Great Britain is currently the most attractive country among all European locations for producing cars. This results from the structural reforms initiated by Margaret Thatcher in the early 1980s, the most significant factor of course being the rearrangement of industrial relations between companies and trade unions. (11 October 1995)

The transformation of industrial relations has led to a matching transformation in our output per worker. In 1979 British industry was approximately 35–50 per cent less productive than that of France and Germany. Since then, our productivity has grown more rapidly than in most other industrialized countries. After decades of slowing down we managed to raise our rate of growth in productivity in manufacturing from 0.5 per cent per year in the period 1974–9 to an average of 3.9 per cent a year since then. As a result we have been narrowing the gap with our Continental competitors to probably less than 10 per cent now. If we stick with that rate of progress we can overtake them in the next five years. That productivity gap has been one of the most vivid indicators of Britain's relative economic decline during this century and to eliminate it during the lifetime of the next Conservative Government would be a historic achievement.

One of the key features of the British disease was the weakness of British business. Now Britain has 50 per cent more active businesses than in 1979. We have the lion's share of Europe's most successful companies. The *Financial Times*'s survey in 1996 of the top five hundred European companies showed Great Britain having sixteen of the twenty-five most profitable companies and nine out of the largest twenty-five. This is one of the many reasons why London is one of the world's top business centres, rivalled only by New York and Tokyo and certainly ahead of Frankfurt or Paris.

Cycles and Trends

The critics say that it is convenient to measure the British economy now when it is enjoying a healthy recovery but ask about the two painful recessions which we suffered first in 1980–81 and then in 1991–2. One recession may be unfortunate – but doesn't two look like carelessness?

We did make a policy mistake but perhaps not the one that most people think we made. Back in October 1987 there was a massive crash in the world's stock markets. The great crash of 1929 had led to the depression of the 1930s and serious economists around the world worried that people who saw their wealth cut back so sharply might ow retrench and drive us into recession. As a result, economic policy was deliberately relaxed internationally – Western governments printed more money. With the wisdom of hindsight, those fears after the stock-market crash were much exaggerated. That loosening of policy had particularly damaging consequences for us as it happened when a strong recovery was already mature. As a result inflation rose to a peak of 10.9 per cent. Once policy had become that loose a painful tightening was inevitable: it would have happened regardless of whether or not we had joined the Exchange Rate Mechanism in 1990. It is perhaps significant that the biggest single mistake we have made in economic management since 1979 came not from being too tough – as the Opposition always charge – but from being too lax.

The statistics now show that the economy was already growing again before we left the ERM in September 1992. Since then the British economy has enjoyed a stronger recovery than any other major European country after the worldwide slowdown of the early 1990s. Output is now more than 8 per cent above its previous peak and we are on track to continue to enjoy that combination of low inflation and steady growth which governments of all parties have sought since the Second World War and so few have been able to deliver.

An economic cycle is an inescapable part of the workings of any modern economy. What is important is the trend around which the cycle oscillates. Any fair measure of our economic performance has to look at the rate of growth over a complete economic cycle taking recession and recovery together. We can use international measures of the economic cycle to make a fair comparison between the performance of Britain and other countries.

Let us begin by looking at economic cycles from peak to peak. In the economic cycle of 1973–9 Great Britain grew at

1.5 per cent per year per head on average, as against France's 2.3 per cent and Germany's 2.5 per cent. In the next complete cycle, 1979–89, Britain grew by 2.2 per cent, France by 1.6 per cent and Germany by 1.9 per cent. The evidence is clear – our major European competitors suffered a slowing down of their growth rate at the same time as we managed to reverse our downward trend and raise our growth rate above theirs.

We can cross-check this by making the data more up to date and covering the last two full economic cycles from trough to trough. In 1975–82 Great Britain grew by 1.3 per cent, France by 2.3 per cent and Germany by 2.4 per cent. In the next full trough-to-trough cycle, 1982–93, the growth of our GDP per head was 2 per cent as against 1.3 per cent for France and 2 per cent for Germany. Indeed, the only country in the group of seven leading economies to grow faster than us was Japan. For the first time since the Second World War we are now enjoying a record of economic growth significantly better than that of our major European competitors. The year 1997 will be the fifth successive one in which we shall have grown faster than France or Germany. If we stick to our policies we can deliver our aim of doubling living standards over the next twenty-five years.

Taxing and Spending

Those international comparisons reveal something else of great significance. The fast-growing economies of the Far East, and to some extent America, take about 30 per cent of their national income in public spending. The slow-growth economies of Continental Europe take about 50 per cent. In 1979 Britain was close to the European average, but since then we have taken a very different path as we have brought our public spending down towards 40 per cent of national income. At the same time our growth rate has improved so that it is better than the Continent's, though behind that of the Far East. This is hard evidence to support a Conservative's instinctive belief that governments are much less effective in spending money than individuals and businesses. The more government gets in the way, the more our growth rate suffers. That is why our aim is to get public spending clearly below 40 per cent of our national income and to keep it there.

Public expenditure goes above all on two things. The biggest item is social-security payments of approximately £90 billion. Second is pay for people who work in the public sector, which adds up to approximately £80 billion. Between them these two items account for three fifths of all public expenditure, running now at about £270 billion out of an economy of almost £700 billion. Setting aside all the arguments about the spending pledges which the Labour Party has made, the underlying question is very simple. Which party is likely to be better at restraining the rate of growth of social-security and public-sector pay? The answer is obvious and anyone who wishes to pursue the point further simply needs to consult *Hansard* and see the way in which Labour Opposition spokesmen have argued and voted since 1979.

As for taxation, the basic question is again a very straightforward one. Which is the party which believes most clearly in giving individuals the greatest possible scope to decide what to do with their own money? We can be proud of our record in bringing down personal tax rates. If we had simply maintained and indexed the income tax and National Insurance structure we inherited in 1979 a married couple on average male earnings with two children would pay 25.9 per cent of their earnings in income tax and National Insurance. Thanks to the policies of this Government they will pay just 20.7 per cent in 1997–8.

The basic rate of income tax has been cut from 33 per cent in 1979 to 23 per cent in 1997–8. The higher rate of income tax has been cut from an absurd 83 per cent to 40 per cent. A new lower rate of 20 per cent has been introduced and applies to the first £4,100 of taxable income. Moreover, the tax in savings income has been cut to just 20 per cent for basic-rate taxpayers. As a result, already over a quarter of all income-tax payers only pay at the 20 per cent rate. Our aim is to achieve a 20 per cent basic rate for everyone. The critics imagine that these tax cuts have favoured the rich but the share of income tax contributed by the top 10 per cent of taxpayers has actually risen from 35 per cent in 1978–9 to 45 per cent in 1996–7. The number of higher-rate taxpayers has risen from 800,000 then to 2.1 million in 1996–7.

If people are really to provide for themselves and build up businesses for their families, it is important that they do not face a burden of capital taxation. This is a tax which eats the seed-corn. It discourages thrift and encourages people to take money out of business in income rather than by building up its capital value. That is why we are pledged to reducing – and eventually abolishing – capital gains tax and inheritance tax.

The Labour Party claims that we have put up taxes since they left office in 1979. We had to put taxes up in the early 1980s and then again in the early 1990s because of the impact of recession on the public finances. Tax rates under the last Labour Government would have been far higher had they not been artificially depressed by massive government borrowing, averaging 6.75 per cent of national income per year between 1974 and 1979 – as against our average of 2.75 per cent per year. We have brought down the combined burden of taxing and public borrowing by 3 per cent of national income. The basic point is very simple. Only two things push up taxes – recessions and Labour governments.

Feeling Good and Feeling Right

We saw in Chapter 2 that the ultimate object of production is consumption. A free market is supposed to enable us to enjoy higher standards of living. Ultimately we should be able to measure the success of our economic policies in the most direct way possible – increases in living standards. And the figures tell a dramatic story. For a married couple with two children with one earner on average male earnings, annual real take-home pay will have increased by £5,090 in real terms between 1978–9 and 1997–8. The increase will be approximately £1,100 since the last election. In 1996–7 alone the increase is £450 – owing to tax cuts and the benefits of economic growth – with a further increase of £370 expected in 1997–8. By comparison, during the entire five years of the last Labour Government the rise was just £60.

We are so used to economic failure in this country we think that such figures must be too good to be true. That is why we hear that rather uncomfortable expression, the 'feel-good factor', as if our rising prosperity is all due to a binge and tomorrow we will be suffering from the hangover. But people do not feel good unless they feel right, that these improvements in their living standards have been earned and can be sustained. That means that two conditions have to be met. First, has the economy enjoyed an underlying improvement in its perform-ance? All the evidence in this chapter from industrial relations, productivity, and economic growth is that we have. Secondly, can our lower taxes be sustained or are we reducing our taxes today by borrowing more, which will mean we have to face higher taxes tomorrow? Again, the evidence is of a reduction in the Government's underlying deficit. Indeed, we are the only one of the world's major seven economies to have cut the national debt compared to the economy's total output since 1979.

So we can look again at that evidence on living standards, confident that this reflects a solid underlying economic achieve-ment. In the decade to 1971 the income of the average house-hold of working age increased by 19 per cent. In the next decade, up to 1981, it increased by 12 per cent. Yet in the decade to 1991 it rose by 39 per cent – more than in the previous twenty years put together. It shows that if we can deliver greater economic growth and at the same time the Government holds down the amount which it takes from people in taxes, then families begin to reap the benefits as their living standards rise.

Policies

All income groups have been able to participate in this rise in living standards. Those at the bottom of the income scale in 1993–4, the last year for which we have authoritative expenditure analysis, spent considerably more than those at the bottom of the income scale in 1979. In 1979, 59 per cent of the population had an income below the average. If we take that same real income level we find that by 1993–4 only 40 per cent of the population were below it.

There are a whole host of statistics which show how our lives have been transformed since 1979 as we have become more prosperous:

- the number of leisure trips abroad rose from 13 million in 1979 to 34 million in 1994;
- the proportion of households with a video recorder rose from 18 per cent in 1983 to 77 per cent in 1994;
- in 1991, 205,000 houses in England – 1 per cent of the housing stock – lacked basic amenities (one or more of hot and cold water; wash-hand basin; bath/shower; indoor WC; sink). This compares with 910,000 houses – 5 per cent of the housing stock – in 1981.

So we do not just have to feel good about our rising prosperity, we can feel right about it too. These improvements in our living standards are not some temporary fiddle masterminded by extraordinarily ingenious politicians. They are a consequence of an underlying improvement in Britain's growth performance. We are entitled to enjoy the benefits of those improvements in our productivity which we saw earlier and now we are doing so. John Major is right to set us the objective of doubling our living standards over the next twenty-five years: if we carry on getting the basic economic decisions right we can deliver on that goal. Free markets are indeed the route to prosperity.

FIVE

Jobs: Mobility or Equality

We face a choice between two models of capitalism. One option is the free-market model which prizes mobility, flexibility, enterprise and individualism: this is the basis for the policies we have been pursuing since 1979. The second option is the Continental model, espoused by 'New' Labour, which stresses 'social partnership' with stakeholders such as trade unions.

Let us see how these two models measure up against what opinion surveys tell us is the economic issue at the top of the electorate's agenda – unemployment. We saw in the last chapter that many crucial indicators showed a clear deterioration as each economic cycle passed since the Second World War. It is like the story of the old Russian peasant who was asked what the harvest was like and replied 'about average'. When pressed as to what this meant he said 'worse than last year but better than next year'. That certainly applies to unemployment across Europe. But in the last recession we reversed that declining trend and unemployment did not reach as big a figure as during the previous recession. Moreover, after the recession of 1979–81, unemployment kept on rising for another five years. By contrast, as soon as the economy started recovering in 1992, unemployment responded almost immediately and has fallen by a million since its peak in December 1992 to about 7 per cent. The critics write as if we are now facing a long-term shake-out of jobs, but actually that painful but necessary process took place in the first half of the 1980s. This time round, as

31

soon as the economic recovery began the demand for new workers picked up as well. If we measure employment rather than unemployment the comparison is even more stark. We have almost 70 per cent of those of working age in work compared with only 60 per cent of people in the rest of the European Union.

In the words of the Organization for Economic Co-operation and Development, Britain now has one of the 'least regulated labour markets' amongst OECD countries, resulting in a 'steady drop in structural unemployment and a relatively good unemployment record compared with many Continental European countries'. The comparison is stark: less than two million people are unemployed here, as against over three million in France and over four million in Germany. These figures are directly relevant to the policy debate between the two parties. Labour 'modernizers' look to the Continental model: that is why they are committed to a minimum wage, the European Social Chapter, and a 'stakeholder' economy. The evidence is unambiguous. We have a much lower unemployment rate than any other major European economy. Abandoning our policies for theirs looks most unlikely to improve our performance: it will undermine it.

Nor are these differences accidental. They are the result of a deliberate – albeit painful – choice which policy-makers had to make. The essential dilemma is that the more you standardize in the interests of equality, the less able you are to include everyone in the labour market. Peter Lilley has made the point very clearly:

The growing dispersion of earning power is probably the most significant social change affecting the United Kingdom and most other Western countries. The earning power of brawn has not kept pace with that of brain. Some countries, especially the United States, New Zealand, Australia, and the United Kingdom have responded to that phenomenon, which affects all advanced countries, by allowing earnings to reflect the change in productivity of different skill groups. As a result, each of those countries has generally experienced a greater dispersion of earnings but more job creation and a smaller rise in unemployment.

By contrast, other countries – notably on the Continent – have endeavoured to prevent wages from reflecting the changing earnings potential of less-skilled people as we increasingly compete with the Far East and experience the impact of new technology. In those countries, growth in inequality is slower, at the expense of higher unemployment and fewer jobs. (House of Commons, 14 February 1995)

So you can have a higher dispersal of earnings and gain greater employment or you can go for a more standardized distribution of earnings and pay the price in terms of higher unemployment.

This rise in returns to cognitive skills relative to manual skills is further magnified by a social phenomenon known as 'assortative mating' – well-paid women tend to marry well-paid men (it is a phenomenon which can indeed be observed in the Blair household itself). Income distribution in this country usually measures not individuals but families or households. The massive opening up of opportunities in the past twenty years for women has been a major factor in the widening of the income gap between households.

It would be wrong to think that people are then trapped for ever on low incomes. We are a very mobile society. The Institute for Fiscal Studies has shown that individuals in the lowest tenth of incomes in one year saw their incomes rise on average by 25 per cent a year later (from £86 per week in 1991 to £110 in 1992). The lowest income category is not composed of the same individuals as it was the previous year, still less fifteen years ago. And the same goes for people who are in work but on low earnings. The earnings of working men in the bottom fifth in 1979 rose proportionately more over the following fifteen years than those in the top fifth – 42 per cent against a 33 per cent rise.

The proportion of people in the bottom tenth of income who own consumer durables has risen enormously since 1979. For example fewer than a third had a fridge-freezer in 1979. Now the overwhelming majority do. Almost no low-income household in 1979 had a video. Now nearly three quarters do. These figures do not necessarily show that people can buy such consumer durables while they are on such a low income. They actually show something rather different and in its way more encouraging. It is wrong to think that the bottom of the income scale is composed of one fixed group of individuals. Our incomes shift up and down during our lives: there is not some permanently fixed underclass. Anyone who has been a student is likely to have managed on an income down at the bottom of the range but, equally, having left college most students move well up the income range.

Labour seek to suppress mobility in the jobs market. They want to regulate pay and conditions more heavily, to use employment law to make it more difficult to reduce staff, and to strengthen unions by forcing companies to recognize them. Our approach by contrast is to deregulate where possible and to restrain union power. We propose to take this approach further in our fifth term. We are consulting industry on the proposal that the burden of unfair-dismissal regulations should be lessened for small firms. Small firms are deterred from recruiting people by the danger of having to pay excessive sums for severance if the individual does not perform. Allowing them to employ people on flexible terms encourages them to take on more staff. This is the paradox at the heart of the argument. Employment protection in the short term destroys jobs in the long term by making employers reluctant to recruit in the future.

Tony Blair talks about everyone becoming a stakeholder in British society. But the stakeholder agenda actually leads to social exclusion not inclusion. 'Stakeholder' companies increase the rights of insiders with long-term contracts and standard hours relative to outsiders. Traditional marginal groups such as young people or women do much better out of our flexible labour market than they do out of the more regulated arrangements of the Continent.

The evidence of hours worked makes the point very clearly. In Germany 28 per cent of employees work 38 hours and 28 per cent work 40 hours. In France 49 per cent work 39 hours. In Italy 20 per cent work 36 hours and 45 per cent work 40 hours. In Spain 66 per cent work 40 hours. Most employees are working full time and for standard hours. The British picture is very different. The number of hours most frequently worked is 40 hours but that is only by 10 per cent of employees. There is a much wider distribution of the number of hours worked. Britain has many more part-time employees than on the Continent. Our more flexible system makes it more possible for people to tailor the number of hours they work to their personal preferences. Eighty-seven per cent of people working part time do not want or are unavailable for full-time work.

More workers in the UK report themselves to be satisfied with their working hours than on the Continent. In Britain, because we have a much more free and diverse arrangement, you are likely to be able to find a job that roughly matches your personal preferences. By contrast, on the Continent if you do not want to work a standard job doing standard hours, you have to be out of the labour market altogether and unemployed.

In the past twenty years America has created 36 million jobs of which 31 million were in the private sector whereas Europe has created five million jobs of which four million were in the public sector. The Continental model which Labour wish to impose here may have its advantages but it is not socially inclusive and it is not successful at generating jobs.

Insecurity

We are told by the critics that this new flexible labour market means that there is no such thing as a secure long-term job and that we are all having to live with greater degrees of insecurity than ever before. The evidence shows that the story is far more complicated.

Data to 1991 show men can on average expect to hold their current job for about eighteen years while women on average can expect theirs to last twelve years. The estimates for data up to 1982 were nineteen years and thirteen years respectively. While about one third of men are currently in jobs that will last less than five years and only one quarter are currently in jobs that will last twenty years, a majority will have, at some point, a job that lasts for twenty years.

Something is happening, but not what the conventional wisdom says. It looks as if there are two very different types of labour market operating at different stages of our lives (in the jargon, it is 'bimodal'). While we are young we move jobs relatively frequently as our personal circumstances change and as we hunt around for the job which best suits us and similarly employers try to find the employees who best fit their business. People aged under thirty account for 60 per cent of new job engagements and they also account for over 50 per cent of the flows on to the claimant unemployment count. Short-term job-changing does appear to have become more common and short-term jobs have become shorter. The number of jobs a person can expect to have in a lifetime increased from 6.8 in 1975 to 8.4 in 1993. But most of these changes occur before people reach the age of thirty. Moreover these changes are largely driven by employees (surveys show that about two thirds of job separations are voluntary – mostly moves to better jobs but also for college, family, etc.).

If we look at older men, the pattern of the job market looks very different. Two fifths of men aged over fifty had already been in their jobs for over twenty years in 1994 and this was only marginally lower than in 1984. Here is another paradox: the British labour market has both a high level of turnover and long tenure. The high-turnover stage lasts up until approximately the age of thirty and has become rather more volatile and lasts slightly longer than in the past. But by about the age of thirty, people have by and large settled into work arrangements with which they are comfortable. At that point, employers have a strong incentive to keep employees and train and retrain them as their jobs develop. That is a rational economic calculation by both employees and employers. Sixty-eight per cent of the jobs created in the UK since 1993 have been permanent and 41 per cent have been full time. 'Bimodal' is never going to replace 'secure' in the lexicon of the conventional wisdom, but it is a far more accurate picture.

Our labour market is certainly different from the heavily regulated labour markets of the Continent and the real difference is rather interesting – and not quite what we are told by Blair and his followers. Assume that you have a lot of heavy-handed social-protection and employment law of the sort which exists on the Continent and which the Labour Party wishes to impose on us through the Social Chapter. Free-market economic principles would suggest that the effect of such legislation would be to create a much greater incentive for employers to employ people on a temporary basis so they did not have to face the full burden of employment protection. The evidence supports exactly what economic principles would predict. On average across the European Union in 1994, 10.9 per cent of employees were on temporary contracts. Spain – which had both the minimum wage and a high level of employment-protection legislation – has no less than 33.6 per cent of employees on temporary contracts. In France it was 10.9 per cent and in Germany it was 10.2 per cent. In Britain, by contrast, 6.3 per cent of employees were on temporary contracts, one of the lowest proportions in Europe. Those Continental governments explicitly trying to create 'social cohesion' by legislating for more employment protection have ended up driving employers into using labour on an evermore casual basis.

Low Pay: Family Credit versus Minimum Wage

Imagine a group of people serving behind the bar at your local pub and earning say £3 an hour. One might be a student boosting his grant. Perhaps another is a young woman with a husband who has got a good job at the factory but she is earning some extra money to pay for a good holiday. Then there is a single parent struggling to raise two children on her own. Finally, perhaps there is a forty-year-old man who has been made redundant and is earning some money to keep his nonworking wife and two children before he can get back into a well-paid job again. They are all doing the same work and so they are all receiving the same wage. But whether or not that is a living wage depends on their circumstances. That is why the single parent and the forty-year-old father would both be entitled to claim Family Credit to help keep their families. A man with a young family working full time at £3 an hour could receive over £55 a week in Family Credit. Family Credit now goes to over 660,000 low-income families and helps the vast majority of families on low incomes to be better off in work than out of work.

Some of our critics say that Family Credit just subsidizes employers who pay low wages. But a recent study showed that very few employers knew whether their staff were eligible for Family Credit or not, and so could not have pushed wages down to account for it. Family Credit costs almost £2 billion a year, it is true. But it is cheaper to pay someone Family Credit than for them to remain on Income Support – which would be the alternative if a minimum wage destroyed their jobs. And for many people, a low-paid job is a first step towards a better one. Only 12 per cent of people on Family Credit receive it for more than twelve months. And Sir Stanley Kalms of Dixons is fond of pointing out that many of his key managers started out in part-time jobs.

Labour do not like Family Credit. Instead they wish to force employers to pay the minimum wage. It is a striking reminder of the basic difference between the two parties when it comes to the free market. It would become a criminal offence to pay an employee less than the rate fixed as the minimum wage. This is a very clumsy way of dealing with poverty because a high proportion of those on low pay live in households with a higher earner. The Institute for Fiscal Studies calculate that a minimum wage would actually help households in the top third of the income distribution by more than those in the bottom third. So it is much worse targeted than Family Credit. Of the 10 per cent of people with the lowest wages, 95 per cent of them are not in the poorest 10 per cent of households. It does badly therefore at helping poverty and it does even worse when it comes to maintaining jobs.

Let us go back to the pub and consider the assistant cook in the kitchen who has been trained at the local college and is earning £4.50 an hour. Suddenly by law all the staff at the bar get paid say £4 an hour (the trade unions want £4.26). Some of those people previously earning £3 an hour won't actually get that pay rise, they won't get any pay at all. Moreover the cook is going to ask the manager for an increase – perhaps to £5.50 to maintain his differential. As Denis Healey rightly observed, 'Don't kid yourselves – the minimum wage is something on which the unions will build differentials . . . Therefore the minimum wage becomes the floor on which you erect a new tower' (Radio 4, 17 October 1994). Whether the minimum wage is set at £3.50, £3.70 or £4.26 is a largely academic point because once the Healey effect kicks in, many more people start losing their jobs. Even if existing differentials are only half-restored, the Department of Trade and Industry calculates that a £3.50 an hour minimum wage would cost 800,000 jobs and a £4.26 minimum wage over one million jobs. And if Labour tried to get away with the wildly implausible claim that there would be no impact on differentials they will undermine their other claim – to believe in education and training – because they will be saying your pay is no better for having got an NVQ or some GCSEs.

Many of the people affected by the minimum wage work in the public services – it is no accident that the campaign is being run by Rodney Bickerstaff of UNISON, the NHS trade union. Back in 1992 Robin Cook estimated that a minimum wage would cost the NHS £500 million. Local authorities would be hit too and schools would have to pay more for their ancillary staff. Gordon Brown's official position is that there will be no increase in spending on the NHS compared with existing plans under a Labour government apart from £100 million raised by some bogus reduction in management costs. That means that given the cost of the minimum wage to the NHS, one can only assume that Labour intend to reduce spending on patient care so as to direct extra money to members of Mr Bickerstaff's union. This is an extraordinary position and it will be repeated all round the public services. Either Labour will end up increasing their public spending or they will have to cut back services in order to pay public-sector unions more.

From Dole to Dignity

Even though British unemployment is significantly below the European average we obviously want to see it lower still. That is why we introduced the new Jobseeker's Allowance in October 1996 which requires unemployed people to be available for and actively seeking work. It makes clear their obligations as jobseekers and gives the Employment Service the power to apply sanctions if they do not fulfil their obligations: it is a powerful set of tools to prevent people languishing on benefit. A wide range of employment programmes backs it up: Training for Work, Jobclubs, Job Interview Guarantees, Work Trials, Jobplan Workshop, 1–2–1 caseloading, Workwise, the Travel to Interview Scheme and Restart interviews and courses.

We are also dealing with the notorious 'why work' problem to ensure that people are better off in work than out of work. For example, the new Back-to-Work bonus helps people working part time and in receipt of the Jobseeker's Allowance or Income Support to accumulate a tax-free bonus of up to £1,000 payable when they get back into full-time work. Any employer who takes on someone previously unemployed for two years now receives a one-year holiday from their National Insurance contributions. If people take a job after six months out of work they can keep their Housing Benefit at their existing rate for four weeks regardless of their earnings. Partners of JSA claimants can now work for up to twenty-four hours per week without the claimant losing entitlement to benefit, so dealing with the serious problem that if someone is unemployed it may become worth while for their partner to give up work. This is just a small selection of a range of imaginative measures and there are more to come.

It is particularly important to help people who are long-term unemployed. Two thirds of those who become unemployed leave the count within six months but some get stuck. Out of the two million people currently unemployed, approximately 750,000 have been unemployed for more than one year and 450,000 for more than two years. We are now developing the most ambitious range of measures aimed at encouraging people into work that any British Government has ever introduced.

These people may have become demoralized and lost contact with the jobs market altogether. Our new Project Work programme is aimed particularly at people unemployed for more than two years. They get thirteen weeks' intensive help with their job search. If this fails, there is thirteen weeks of job experience, including training grants to employees helping on a community work project. Participants receive an allowance of £10 a week on top of their benefit entitlement. It gets them back in the habit of daily work and is also a real test of availability for work which catches those who have jobs in the black economy. We now intend to extend Project Work to approximately 100,000 of the long-term unemployed in carefully selected parts of the country.

We also propose to harness the energies of the private and voluntary sectors to help find jobs for the long-term unemployed and also for single parents who want to work through our new Parent-Plus initiative. They can act as specialized employment agencies with payments by results. The evidence from America where this approach has been tried suggests that the results can be very good indeed.

Long-term unemployment has fallen by 600,000 since its peak back in 1986. The policies set out in this chapter, and only such policies, can enable us to continue to bring the figure down.

SIX

Schools: Choice or Uniformity

British Governments come to power at different dates in different departments. Governments have to set priorities and while intense political battles are being fought over some areas of policy, others may be left untouched for years.

There was a burst of activity in education policy when we introduced the Assisted Places Scheme in 1980 to enable children from low-income households to enjoy the benefits of an independent education. The pupils in the scheme recorded pass rates of over 94 per cent in both GCSE and A levels in 1995, which makes its £117 million cost in 1996–7 good value for money. Labour are pledged to get rid of it (a vivid example of the conflict between equality and mobility which we discussed in the last chapter).

For most of the 1980s, however, the big battles were fought elsewhere. The main story in education was expansion. The proportion of adults with no academic qualification whatsoever has fallen from 55 per cent in 1979 to 32 per cent in 1994. Twenty-five per cent of adults have GCSE grades A–C in 1994 compared with 14 per cent in 1979. The proportion of adults with A levels has more than doubled, from 5 per cent in 1979 to 11 per cent in 1994.

In the 1979–80 academic year there were 795,000 students in higher education; in 1994–5 the figure was more than double at 1,701,000. This expansion spells the end of the old elitist British university structure. In the old days we spent a lot per student, including a generous maintenance grant. That high level of spending per student was only possible for a system aimed at a tiny elite of students: it acted as a barrier to expansion. The increase in student numbers has been associated with a change in the pattern of student support. Nearly two million student-loan accounts will have been created by 1997–8 with some £4 billion of loans outstanding. That is a massive contribution to student welfare: it is inconceivable taxpayers, often on modest incomes themselves, would have been willing to pay it all outright as grants.

Raising Standards

Class sizes fell during the 1980s yet at the same time there was increasing worry about what was going on in the classroom. Indeed, there is little evidence of any correlation between class size and educational achievements. (It is a reliable test of good public policy that anyone who focuses on inputs, particularly money, is doing so to avoid facing the real challenge of raising the quality of the outputs.)

Raising standards in schools is one of the Government's highest priorities. An extremely ambitious reform agenda is now being put into place by Gillian Shephard. It is of enormous significance in its own right and also exemplifies one of the central themes running through this book – what should we share as a community and where should individualism reign.

Conservatives recognize that our ties are far more than merely economic. Our shared historic culture is the most powerful force for national integration. Education can give everyone and anyone access to our literary and historical tradition. It is a sad irony that those progressive thinkers so keen to criticize Thatcherite individualism and the privatization of industry – where it makes obvious sense – have themselves encouraged the privatization of our culture. Look at the changes in a typical school curriculum over the past thirty years – one can see the fracturing of our literary tradition as the trivial and the meretricious jostle alongside the great. Similarly, a sense of the shape of our history has been lost, to be replaced by a miscellany of themes and special subjects. No longer can we be confident that someone emerging from our schools will have come across the novels of Charles Dickens or know who Winston Churchill was. That cultural disinheritance is real deprivation. Look too at the hostility among trendy educationists to school uniforms or a school assembly, the things which bring a school together as a community. The battle for educational standards and strong schools is now perhaps the most important single battle for a Conservative to fight.

The National Curriculum aims to ensure that pupils have a minimum shared understanding of their own nation's language, literature, and history, as well of course as the essential skills of mathematics, science, etc. That is the real way of ensuring some national sense of community rather than through heavy-handed intervention in the operation of the economy.

But 'community' does not mean much unless it is embodied within actual institutions which transmit values and shape people. Here again there is a clear division between the parties. For the Labour Party, the educational institution which matters above all is the local education authority (LEA). Our policy is to give schools the greatest possible freedom and independence. All the evidence is that the head teacher is crucial in shaping the character of the school but she cannot do that if an LEA is breathing down her neck.

We have shifted much more budgetary power to individual schools through our local management of schools initiative. Over one thousand schools have gone further and enjoy full independence from local-authority control as grant-maintained schools. (Indeed nearly one in five of our state secondary pupils are now educated in grant-maintained schools and comprise no less than 46 per cent of 200 schools recently identified by the Chief Inspector as either excellent or very good.) LEAs know that if they treat an individual school badly then it can leave their control altogether and become grant-maintained instead. Labour want to bring grant-maintained schools for all practical purposes under the control of the very local authorities they have tried to escape. We want to move in the opposite direction, as far as possible – so that all schools recognize that their funding depends on satisfied parents, not local planners.

Probably the most important single measures we have taken to raise educational standards have been the introduction of rigorous and consistent testing at ages seven, eleven, fourteen and sixteen, together with publication of the results. We now intend to take this a stage further and introduce a baseline assessment of children's skills when they enter school at five. When we can trace an individual's attainment all through their school years there is no need to get into the blind alley of sociological attempts to construct indices of deprivation and value-added by schools. Instead we can see for each stage what a school starts with and what it has achieved during the years the pupil is with them. The publication of test results – so welcomed by parents and so opposed by Labour and the teacher unions – has also proved to be an essential spur to schools to improve their performance.

In addition we have new tougher inspections by OFSTED and the publication of their results in a frank and readable form instead of the gobbledegook of the old HMI reports. These new inspections should cover every school every four years as against an average of one visit every fifty years under the old regime. The new inspections are identifying schools which are clearly failing their pupils – 160 out of the 8,000 inspected so far. Remedial action has to be taken. Either those schools have to show clear improvement within two years or we will move towards closing them down.

We have also had the guts to publish the uncomfortable evidence that 20 per cent of our children leave school without achieving basic literacy. That is simply not acceptable. We have therefore launched new literacy and numeracy centres aimed at helping teachers to teach more effectively. Over five years, up to 2,000 primary schools – one in ten – will be helped directly by this scheme and the results spread even more widely.

We are also trying to strengthen professional standards in the teaching profession. Gillian Shephard has rightly said: 'None of us can be satisfied when OFSTED tells us that one lesson in five is not up to standard.' Professional standards and professional ethos are absolutely vital, but sadly what went wrong during the 1960s and 1970s was that the profession became inward-looking. It fell a prey to educational dogma which was not supported by any empirical evidence. The evidence is now coming in that whole-class teaching works and that traditional ways of teaching reading are the most effective. Of course, we need professional standards but it must be, to use the newly fashionable expression, evidence-based pedagogy.

In return teachers are entitled to the fullest possible support in ensuring that they can maintain discipline in the classroom and dealing with the problems of drugs, truancy, and bullying which must not be allowed to blight our schools. We are legislating to strengthen schools' disciplinary powers. They will be able to detain unruly pupils after hours without getting parental permission. They should be able to exclude unruly pupils from school for up to forty-five days per year. They should be entitled to take a parent's willingness to sign a home–school contract as a relevant criterion for new entrants to the school. And we are putting more effort into ensuring that there is proper teaching available outside school for the disruptive pupils who have been excluded.

We have opened up a debate on educational standards by providing much more information than ever available before. Now we know what makes a school a success, as the progressive dogmas of twenty years ago have been refuted by the evidence.

Choice and Diversity

Once head teachers have greater scope to shape the character of their own schools then parents have the scope to make genuine choices. By getting rid of the old fixed catchment areas and introducing open enrolment we have in effect created a paperless voucher within the public sector. Schools which attract more pupils will get more funding and parents can choose which school to apply for on behalf of their child. This is not some new piece of ideology. The power of parental choice interacting with the importance of the individual head teacher was recognized by the Royal Commission on the State of Popular Education in 1861:

It is a subject of wonder how people so destitute of education as labouring parents commonly are, can be such just judges as they also commonly are of the effective qualifications of a teacher. Good school buildings and the apparatus of education are found for years to be practically useless and deserted when, if a master chanced to be appointed who understands his work, a few weeks suffice to make the fact known, and his school is soon filled, and perhaps found inadequate to the demand of the neighbourhood, and a separate girls' school or infant school is soon found to be necessary.

That is a pretty good summary of the role of the head teacher, the strength of parent power, and the relative unimportance of levels of spending on buildings and equipment.

If parents are to exercise choice then it becomes even more important to give them useful information on which to base their choices.

Choice and information empower parents on what one might regard as the demand side of the equation. Equally it is important to give them a variety of schools to choose from – to liberalize on the supply side. The trend through the 1960s and 1970s was to eliminate diversity. The last Labour Government deliberately destroyed direct-grant grammar schools in a wilful act of educational vandalism. Technical schools, which had been envisaged by R. A. Butler as the third element of secondary schooling alongside grammar schools and secondary moderns, were discouraged and largely disappeared. We are working flat out to reverse that trend. The number of specialist schools is increasing at last – there are 30 language colleges, and 151 technology colleges as well as 15 city technology colleges and of course 163 grammar schools with their long-standing tradition of excellence. To extend choice and diversity further, we now propose to:

- encourage existing schools to put forward proposals to become grammar schools;
- give all schools the power if they wish to select a proportion of their pupils by general ability or aptitude in particular subjects, without needing central approval;
- extend the specialist schools programme to cover sports colleges and arts colleges; to set up more technology and language colleges, and to help existing technology and language colleges to keep developing their specialist subjects.

It is not just a matter of making it easier for existing schools to shape their own characters. We also need to make it easier for new schools to be established and for popular ones to expand. One of the sad lessons from the Government's initiative on city technology colleges is that many Labour LEAs are deeply hostile to new schools being established outside their control and will do whatever they can to obstruct them – including refusing permission for technology colleges to set up on unused school sites. It is still far too difficult to set up a new school in this country. And if a school is popular but does not wish to expand further it should spawn a new sister school. At the same time failing schools can drag on for far too long before they are taken over by 'new management', perhaps drawn from a successful school nearby, or closed down entirely. To get good schools we need more births, deaths and marriages among them.

Nursery Vouchers

Serious and effective educational reform comes from bringing pressure on both the demand side and the supply side. The clearest and most topical example of this is the nursery voucher. For the first time we will be guaranteeing three terms of good-quality nursery education for every four-year-old. The voucher will be worth £1,100 per child. The scheme will mean an extra £390 million flows into nursery education over the next three years.

The conventional way forward, which the Labour Party supports, would simply have been to require every state infant school to open a class for four-year-olds. If you wished to carry on sending your child to the local pre-school playgroup or voluntary or private nursery, you would have got no help. The direction of public financing would have favoured the public sector as the monopoly provider and the existing diverse pattern of provision would have been threatened. But we have been much more imaginative. Parents can spend their voucher on the nursery education of their choice – be it a state school or an independent provider. The only requirement is that the nursery be inspected to establish that there is a basic minimum educational standard. Existing independent and charitable providers will not be at any disadvantage and indeed new providers will be encouraged to enter the market.

We are for the first time guaranteeing to pay for the nursery education of every four-year-old, yet without any bias in favour of the public sector. It will be entirely a matter of parents choosing what they think is in the best interests of their children. It is an exciting example of the power of the voucher in social policy – and it has been opposed throughout by the Labour Party.

SEVEN

Order and Law

A Loss of Virtue?

Are we experiencing what one book has entitled 'a loss of virtue'? And if so, what can government do about it? Perhaps no questions are so important, and none more difficult for a politician to address, because we have no special claims to moral superiority. Moreover politicians have to formulate public policy without losing sight of the basic point that these are matters of right and wrong for which each individual has to take responsibility.

The critics normally muddle up two completely inconsistent arguments. First, they claim that terrible changes are indeed happening and the blame lies with the free market – a claim which we have already studied. Then if ever a Conservative dares suggest that there is a problem we are accused of whipping up a 'moral panic' and told that really there is not a problem at all. Yet clearly something is happening and we need to try to be clear what it is.

Several different phenomena convey this sense of social disorder: the increase in the number of single-parent families, particularly young never-married mothers of whom there were 80,000 in 1971, 170,000 in 1981 and 440,000 in 1991; the unqualified, unskilled young men who find it difficult to hold down a job; the rise in delinquency and crime, particularly among young people. If we look at these phenomena of family breakdown, unemployability, and crime, we see that young men aged fifteen to twenty-five are the crucial link. They are getting the teenage girls pregnant yet the women – often understandably – have no desire to marry them. It is their long-term unemployment which causes the greatest instability, particularly in inner city areas. And half of all crime is likely to be committed by men under twenty-one.

Most serious social problems can be traced back to these young males, who have lost the structure to their lives that came from serving in the armed forces, traditional apprenticeships, and the burden of being breadwinners for their own family as soon as they left the parental home. Instead they now lead chaotic, impulsive lives as they take a decade to shift from being dependent on their parents to having family responsibilities of their own.

We know quite a lot about these juvenile offenders: they tend to be of low intelligence, hyperactive, and impulsive; their parents have supervised them poorly with harsh and erratic discipline; their parents are disproportionately likely to be separated and their mother to have given birth as a teenager; their parents and siblings are themselves more likely to have a criminal record.

A lot of young men will engage in a small amount of crime and a small number of young men will engage in a lot of crime. (Less than 1 per cent of males born in 1973 who were convicted of four or more offences by the age of seventeen accounted for 40 per cent of all convictions for that age group.) The peak age of offending, eighteen, actually coincides with a peak of affluence for these young men because they are likely to be in unskilled manual jobs (although their long-term income prospects are not good, their disposable income may well be higher than that of their peers who are staying on at school or in higher education). Most of them eventually give up crime and settle down. The biggest single reason for abandoning crime is pressure from a girlfriend or wife. As James Q. Wilson has observed, 'Marriage not only involves screening people for their capacity for self-control, but also provides an inducement

– the need to support a mate, care for a child, and maintain a house – that increases that capacity.' Even after adjusting for all other factors, married men are less likely to be engaged in crime. They also say they stop because penalties are tougher for older, more 'professional' criminals.

Some pundits argue that the problem with these young men is that they have become shamelessly individualistic loners. We have all heard politically correct commentators on the radio and the television saying that all these men are doing is putting into practice Mrs Thatcher's remark that 'there is no such thing as society'. But as we noted in Chapter 3, nineteenth-century Britain experienced dramatic reduction in rates of illegitimacy, drunkenness and crime and this 'remoralization' occurred at the high point of free trade and limited government. Moreover, these young men are sociable and gregarious: juvenile crime is group crime. It is the older, 'professional' burglar for example who is much more likely to be alone. They stop offending when they stop going around in groups and settle down into the bourgeois lifestyle which cynics have been mocking for the past thirty years.

The challenge is to create a legal and institutional framework which helps these people come to adulthood. We fail them if they can avoid ever having to confront the consequences of their actions. That is to trap them in an infantile state in which authority is never exercised, facts are never faced and self-destructive behaviour is tolerated until it is too late. Getting this sort of message through to children by preaching at them is a pretty hopeless task, but they should be able to experience these lessons through their own experience of institutions which are both benign and authoritative. It is very difficult for the local institutions which really can help share people's lives – schools, children's homes, training schemes, the criminal justice system – to exercise authority if they are systematically being turned into powerless recipients of instructions which come down from a central authority. That is why 'civic Conservatism' is about giving back to those institutions powers they lost when big central government wrecked social policy just as surely as it wrecked economic policy during the post-war period. At the same time as big government was planning local institutions into powerlessness it was also manufacturing new rights in ever-more ambitious legislation. Let us look at some of the ways in which we can restore the balance back towards 'order' and law.

The Civic Agenda

Schools need to be able to exercise discipline without being squeezed between the individual rights of parents and the over-arching powers of LEAs. We are proposing a new legal framework for detention to allow schools to detain pupils after school irrespective of consent from the parents. Schools would also have greater flexibility in excluding pupils for fixed periods – giving them a total of forty-five days over the school year. We are also legislating to remove obstacles to the wider use of home–school contracts by allowing oversubscribed schools to insist on such contracts as an admission criterion. And the Department for Education is also looking at new ways of reinforcing and strengthening existing arrangements to tackle the problem of truancy, which is often a first step towards juvenile crime.

Local authorities often have good knowledge of the particular problems of a community and are being given greater powers to deal with the problems they are aware of. The Home Office used to advise local authorities that they did not have a power to pass by-laws aimed at preventing nuisance to residents on private property. They have now concluded that the 1972 Local Government Act does actually allow local authorities power to make such by-laws.

Between 2 per cent and 10 per cent of tenants on any given council estate have been the subject of complaint. This is a serious problem affecting the quality of life of millions of people. A package of measures in the recent Housing Act strengthened public, and in some cases private, landlords' powers to evict nuisance tenants, speed up the procedures to do so, and provide stronger powers to restrain such behaviour. Guidance has now been issued to local authorities on how to make best use of the courts to obtain speedier convictions. Noise can be a particular problem on such estates and our recent noise legislation will improve the effectiveness of neighbour-noise control in all residential property.

It is also important to re-establish a police presence in public areas. One of the ways we can do this is by increasing use of closed-circuit television, which can have dramatic effects on crime rates – down 55 per cent in Bedford city centre, for example. Technology can take us even further by, in effect, taking the old blue police box and computerizing it so that people have instant access to a police station if they see trouble. And best of all we need more police officers on the beat. Since 1979 the number of police officers has been increased by 16,000 with another 5,000 to come, and there are 17,000 more civilians to take the burden of paperwork which was keeping policemen off the front line. Police officers with close local knowledge are particularly valuable and Michael Howard is encouraging new forms of local voluntary policing with more special constables, community police officers, and parish constables appointed on a part-time basis by an individual parish council. They can all help reclaim public spaces for law-abiding citizens.

There are also common-sense measures which private organizations ought to be free to take. In the past few years they have increasingly been advised they may be subject to legal challenge if they try to take obvious measures to protect themselves. Shopkeepers plagued by a group of shoplifters working in a town centre are not sure whether they can circulate photographs of members of the gang and ban them from all their shops. If a gang has been gathering in a shopping centre, the owners did not in the past have the power to ban them from the premises, but now they can. And last but not least victims and the police should be free from prosecution for reasonable use of force.

Then there are the children in trouble who have fallen under the supervision of social services or the probation service, or been placed in children's homes. We know from the behaviour of Lib–Lab councils what they think should be done in these circumstances: they think that young tearaways should be sent on foreign trips to bolster their self-esteem. But free gifts paid for out of the public purse do not bolster anyone's self-esteem. Instead they send out the perverse message that if you get into trouble and start misbehaving you will be given a treat. And they make the average law-abiding citizen, carefully saving to pay for his child to go on holiday, feel as if he is being made a fool of. That is why the Home Secretary had to step in to make it clear that such trips should not be allowed.

The criminal justice system needs to be able to deal with delinquents toughly, clearly and efficiently. It has not always succeeded in the past. It can operate like a classic bad parent – unpredictable, wayward, by turns lenient and harsh. Juvenile delinquents are short-termists with no sense of the long-term consequences of their actions. That means they need to experience a criminal justice system which responds rapidly and firmly to their misbehaviour. Instead, too many so-called reforms have made the system evermore long-drawn-out and incomprehensible. The process between being caught throwing the brick through the window or mugging the old lady and the final punishment can be too long and complicated. Cautioning for example can be very effective at first in keeping people out of the courts but its effectiveness rapidly declines. Only 11 per cent of those with no criminal history prior to a caution were convicted within the next two years. But for those who received a caution having already been cautioned once before, 22 per cent went on to be convicted within the next two years. And for those with two or more previous cautions the rate went up to 45 per cent. So cautions are useful but they must be used sparingly.

The court hearing itself, which should be charged with significance, can easily degenerate into triviality. Seeing a teenage tearaway appear in court for the first time chastened and worried and then leave a quarter of an hour later with a cheeky smile of relief as he discovers it does not mean anything at all, gives a depressing sense that one of our last chances of rescuing him has been lost. Sometimes the courts will impose a community sentence: we have issued new standards so that they are rigorous and demanding. In Scotland everybody on a community sentence has to wear a uniform clearly identifying that this is what they are doing. Another way of literally keeping tabs on offenders is through tagging. Tagging is particularly effective for dealing with young people who are likely to commit offences at predictable times such as at weekends or after pub closing times. Properly used tagging is a very effective extra part of the criminal justice system and we are proposing new powers to extend it. For the really tough juvenile offenders aged down to twelve we are now proposing to set up secure training centres.

Ministers are working to speed up the criminal justice system so that young offenders are punished for their crimes as quickly as possible. The Government is working to reduce delays and cut excessive paperwork. Justice must be quicker, it must be more visible and there needs to be a strengthening of police powers with a greater range of penalties available for police and the courts. That approach is now delivering results.

Serious Crime

Much of this chapter has focused on the behaviour of the young tearaway because these are the problems that afflict us most. But equally we need to ensure we are tough with older professional criminals and those who commit violent crime. The past thirty years have seen the criminal justice system swing too far in their favour. Michael Howard has summarized the problem very clearly:

A guilty suspect who ten or fifteen years ago might readily have confessed, pleaded guilty, and been convicted without further ado, may now be far more likely to contest a case and try his luck in the system.

He is less likely to cooperate at the police station. He is more likely to challenge the evidence against him, and to seek access to a whole range of material to discover possible ways of doing so. He demands copies of all conceivably relevant documents to help patch up or indeed to concoct a defence, or in the hope of hitting upon an informant who has to be protected by dropping the case. (Bramshill Police College, 11 July 1996)

That is why Michael Howard has been bravely and steadily taking steps to restore fairness to the criminal justice system. Some of the measures have already been passed into law. Now courts can draw inferences from silence on the part of suspects. We are proposing a new regime for prosecution and defence disclosure to stop time-wasting fishing expeditions by defence lawyers. A new offence has been introduced of witness intimidation. Where there has been a miscarriage of justice due to such intimidation there is now a power to allow the courts to set aside acquittals and to order a retrial. The Law Commission is looking at relaxing the rules on admitting hearsay evidence and also to admit more evidence on previous convictions.

We now propose to restore fairness in sentencing. The maximum sentence for trafficking in hard drugs, taking a gun to the scene of a crime and attempted rape have all been increased to life imprisonment. But the public is rightly incensed when prisoners are released automatically after they have served only half or two thirds of their sentence. The Government intends to scrap automatic early release from prison and allow prisoners who behave well and cooperate to earn a small amount of time off their sentence – the rest should serve their sentences in full.

In 1994, the average sentence for a first-time conviction for domestic burglary was only 16.2 months in the Crown Courts and 3.7 months in the magistrates' courts. Even after three or more convictions the average sentence only rose to 18.9 months, and after seven or more convictions to 19.4 months. Twenty-eight per cent of convicted burglars with seven or more convictions were not even sent to prison. In the magistrates' courts the figure was 61 per cent. Under the Government's new proposals, anyone convicted on three separate occasions of domestic burglary would automatically be sent to prison for three years. And anyone convicted on three separate occasions for dealing in hard drugs would automatically go to prison for seven years.

A sample of serious violent and sexual offenders taken from 1994 showed that only one in twenty of those convicted of a second such crime actually got life. In 1994, 434 offenders were convicted of rape or attempted rape – only twelve got life. Unless they do get life these offenders *must* be released when they have served two thirds of their sentence – even if the authorities have every reason to believe that they will reoffend. This does not give the public the protection it needs. We propose that anyone convicted of a second serious violent or sexual offence would automatically get life. Such criminals would then only be released if they no longer posed a danger to the public. In these cases the trial judge, not ministers, would set the tariff – the minimum period to be served for retribution and deterrence. Once the tariff had been served the parole board would decide whether or not it was safe to release the offender.

Daring to be Optimistic

Too often we talk about morality, order, law, as if it is just obvious that everything is going to the dogs. There is certainly a problem with the transition of young men from their parental home to a home where they themselves are responsible parents, as we mentioned earlier. But it does not follow that we can generalize about the rest of society too. Tony Blair has made the extraordinary claim that our society is 'fundamentally wrong' (*Today* programme, 21 October 1996). It is his pessimism which is wrong.

The social scientists have come up with an ingenious experiment to measure standards of public morality: they drop wallets with cash and an address and measure how many are returned. *Reader's Digest* recently repeated this exercise in various towns in Great Britain, dropping wallets containing £30, an address and a photograph of a family. Out of the 80 wallets which they dropped, 52 were returned – a score of 65 per cent. In a similar survey which they conducted in America, 67 per cent were returned. In a test of eighteen different Continental European cities the rate was 58 per cent. Most people do still live their lives within a clear moral structure.

Moreover, although some social rules may weaken, others can emerge and be reinforced. Attitudes to drink driving, for example, have been transformed. In 1979 there were 1,790 fatalities from road accidents involving illegal alcohol levels. And what do you think the figure was for 1995? 580. Another statistic confirms the same story. In 1979, 41,000 drivers in road-injury accidents were tested for alcohol and of them, 14,000 failed – a failure rate of 34 per cent. In 1995, 119,000 drivers were tested and 7,500 failed – a failure rate of 6 per cent. A combination of tougher penalties, active police campaigns, and effective advertising, has created a sterner popular view of drinking and driving than we had before.

When it comes to the specifics of crime and policing we are also beginning to understand, or relearn old lessons, about what works and what doesn't. In New York they have focused on enforcing the laws on elementary offences to re-create a sense of public order. And the result? A 40 per cent fall in the crime rate in three years and homicides at their lowest level for over thirty years. British police forces are now trying to do the same, for example, in Hampshire Police's 'Enforcing the Peace' initiative. At the same time the police are also much more active in going for known burglars: initiatives such as Operation Bumble Bee have yielded significant results. Michael Howard has taken the lead too in pressing for tough prison sentences, as the evidence is that prison works. One study interviewed a group of prisoners aged twenty-one to forty-six who were due for release. The thought uppermost in many of their minds was the wish not to return to prison. The most frequently given reason for wanting to give up crime was the fear of prison.

Policies

The combination of tougher policing, the enhanced fear of prison, and commercial pressures from insurers are having an effect. There are two ways of measuring this: through offences notified to the police (recorded crime); and through the British Crime Survey of people's actual experience regardless of whether it is notified to the police. Recorded crime in England and Wales in the twelve months to June 1996 was 10 per cent lower than three years earlier, that is, approximately half a million fewer offences. The 1996 British Crime Survey showed the smallest-ever increase. Both measures showed falls in crimes against property, which accounts for 93 per cent of all recorded crime. There were increases in violence against the person, particularly domestic and acquaintance violence, where patterns of tolerance and reporting are shifting. Crime is still far too high but it is not on an inevitable upward trend. The pessimists are not always right.

EIGHT

The Constitution: Reform or Turmoil

One way to choose between political parties is simply to compare their policies and newspaper pundits produce neat lists of Conservative and Labour policies to help us do just that. But this fails to capture a whole dimension of politics – decisions about priorities. Governments have limited legislative space and political energy. They have to decide what to do first. If Tony Blair were Prime Minister, constitutional change would be the highest priority of his Government. The list of constitutional proposals which Labour has assembled is extraordinarily ambitious and they alone would absorb most of the energies of a Labour Government for several years. Indeed, this is exactly what happened under the last Labour Government, which got completely bogged down in legislation on devolution. Now Labour proposes to do the following:

- hold a referendum and then legislate for a Scottish Parliament and a Welsh Assembly;
- establish a new regional tier of government as a prelude to elected regional assemblies after regional referendums;
- remove hereditary peers from the House of Lords and then consult on a new form of second chamber;
- start work on a Bill of Rights and incorporate the European Convention on Human Rights into UK law;
- introduce a Freedom of Information Act;
- hold a referendum on electoral reform.

Policies

It is no surprise that Tony Blair has claimed that Labour has 'the most extensive package of constitutional change ever proposed' (Glasgow, 11 November 1994). At least they solemnly assured us in their draft manifesto that they 'have no plans to replace the monarchy' (though several of their front-bench spokesmen do envisage a big reduction in the powers of the monarch, in effect creating a presidential function exercised by the Speaker of the House of Commons).

What is extraordinary about Labour's programme is that it is so ambitious and yet does not appear to have been rigorously thought through at all. There is no serious Labour Party document which explains their overall constitutional agenda and how it hangs together. The Labour supporter who has had the honesty to recognize this problem is Professor David Marquand. Perhaps because he served as a Labour MP when they were in office he approaches these issues with rather more realism and frankness than his successors:

Labour is committed to a substantial programme of constitutional change – a Scottish Parliament, embryonic regional authorities in England, a Bill of Rights, the extrusion of the hereditary peerage from the House of Lords, a referendum on proportional representation. It is a formidable list; and the party leadership can legitimately claim that it goes further than any major British party has proposed since the First World War. Yet apart from the Scottish Parliament, there is a curiously makeshift air about it. No coherent vision informs it; no spine of theory or analysis holds it together or links it to the rest of Labour's programme. Above all, its implications for the fundamentals of British statehood – and theirs for it – do not seem to have been explored . . . In England, Labour has embraced reform – in so far as it has embraced it at all – as a concession to individualist chic, rather than as a precondition of social cohesion and public purpose. (David Marquand, *Guardian*, 18 September 1995)

That remark about 'individualist chic' is particularly significant. One of the themes of this book has been that we need to recognize what ties us together as a nation, such as the shared culture and history which our schools should transmit. Something else which ties us together is an extraordinarily stable constitutional framework, with which we are so familiar that it has become part of our identity. Labour imagine we are tied together by redistributive taxation and a set of constitutional contracts with our fellow citizens to be enforced by judges. That is why they would so casually meddle with an elaborate interlocking mechanism which has served us well. This is not to claim that the British constitution is some perfect God-given gift to be preserved unchanged. Only the most absurd reactionary could possibly maintain that it can or should remain fixed for evermore. The question is whether we approach it with the impatience of some post-war town planner and tear down the fabric we have inherited, or whether we instead settle for a judicious programme of improvements. Conservatives have introduced many practical improvements since 1979 and there are more to come. The crucial difference between us and Labour is that we have a better understanding of the underlying working logic of our institutions and therefore how best to reform them. Labour's proposals are deeply muddled: that is why they would create such turmoil.

We will see the difference between incoherent radicalism and practical reform in three crucial areas where there is a legitimate public desire for improvements in the way that we are governed: devolution and decentralization; Parliamentary reform; and more openness.

Devolution and Decentralization

Both Scotland and Wales are enjoying an economic resurgence as they shift from traditional rust-belt industries to dynamic new ones. Thirty per cent of Europe's personal computers are made in Scotland and Edinburgh is a great financial centre. Wales is a massive producer of cars, television sets, and microchips. As a result we see a new self-confidence. Conservatives understand this and welcome it. We are not the English Nationalist Party but the Unionist Party, which is a very different thing

Policies

– a party which believes in the Union between the distinct countries which make up the United Kingdom.

This strong sense of Welsh and Scottish identity gets powerful economic and cultural expression and we are ensuring that the political system also adapts to it. We have recently introduced the very significant change of enabling the Scottish Grand Committee, of which all Scottish MPs are members, to call British Ministers to account in Scotland. Already the Chancellor of the Exchequer has participated in the Scottish Grand Committee when it met in Aberdeen. The Prime Minister himself took part in the debate held at Dumfries. This is a far more flexible device than a Scottish Assembly, which would not be able to call Ministers of the UK Parliament to take part. We now propose to introduce similar arrangements in Wales and Northern Ireland.

Labour's devolution proposals are among the most confused, unworkable policies ever put before the British electorate by a serious political party. They want Scotland to elect its Parliament by proportional representation, while Wales should elect its Assembly by first-past-the-post. A Scottish Parliament is supposed to have a quota to ensure equal representation of men and women, though they have not explained how this is to be compatible with a functioning democracy. Nor do they explain if the Secretaries of State for Scotland and Wales, who currently act as powerful advocates for those countries at the British Cabinet table, would any longer have any useful function. It is not clear whether there are to be completely new governments for Scotland and Wales with their own Prime Ministers or whether these are merely legislative assemblies. Mr Ron Davies, Labour's spokesman on Wales, has assured us that their 'policy is clear' though he did then add 'and it will become clearer'. Any one of these muddles should be enough to sink a policy in normal conditions. But the list above does not even include the two worst problems.

Labour's most controversial proposal is to vest a Scottish Parliament with the power to increase income tax in Scotland, initially by up to three pence in the pound. That represents an additional tax bill of more than £6 a week for the average Scottish household. As Michael Forsyth has pungently pointed out: 'They are proposing discriminatory taxation which would result in an individual working in Dumfries taking home a smaller pay packet than someone doing the same job for the same wage in Durham.' Labour respond that in theory a Scottish Parliament could levy lower taxes than in England. It is inconceivable however that, in Michael Forsyth's words, 'English MPs could be expected to continue voting 35 per cent more money to Scotland than to their own constituencies, only to see it used to finance tax cuts north of the border.'

Then there is the so-called West Lothian question, first raised by Tam Dalyell when he was the Member of Parliament for that constituency. How could Scottish MPs continue to legislate for England when English MPs have no jurisdiction for Scotland? This gets to the heart of the British constitutional settlement. After all, the general elections of 1964 and 1974 saw a Conservative majority in England which was offset by Labour majorities in Scotland and Wales. What Labour want to do is to keep those Scottish votes so that they can impose socialism in England whilst at the same time keeping the English out of all matters affecting Scotland. It is playing with fire.

At the moment Scotland is over-represented at Westminster – there are seventy-two Scottish MPs whereas there would be approximately fifty-nine if they had equal representation with the rest of the United Kingdom. Indeed, Northern Ireland had fewer than its proportionate number of MPs when it had its own separate assembly. If Labour were as high-minded as they claim they might show some willingness to recognize this, but unfortunately for them nearly a fifth of all Labour MPs come from Scotland. If there were a Labour Government we would have a Chancellor, a Foreign Secretary and a Chief Whip all from Scotland and they are not going to do anything to weaken that power base. So the extraordinarily undemocratic proposal is that Scotland should have proportionately more MPs than the rest of the United Kingdom and its own assembly and Scottish MPs would be able to vote on English matters in the Westminster Parliament. This is explosive stuff. It is not a serious attempt to hold the Union together – it would risk blowing it apart.

Labour have tried to deal with this problem by appearing to offer the same devolution to the regions of England as they are offering to Scotland and Wales. They propose to set up regional tiers of government above current county councils and staffed with their appointees. They would then, where there was popular demand, hold a referendum on whether these should become democratically elected regional assemblies. As Stephen Dorrell has observed: 'I know of no problem to which my constituents think a directly elected East Midlands Parliament is the solution.'

The irony is that there is a problem here. People do feel that too many decisions are taken at remote levels of authority, far removed from their practical local concerns. There is a demand for credible decentralization. We can only deliver that if we work with the grain of our history and our political culture. We do not have a strong sense of regional identity – apart perhaps from the south-west and north-east of England. But what we do have is a strong sense of local identity and of neighbourhood. Labour's plans take us in exactly the wrong direction: they would actually weaken local powers. A Scottish Parliament, Welsh Assembly, or English regional assemblies would encroach on decisions taken by local authorities. As Lord Tonypandy, former Labour MP and Speaker of the House of Commons put it: 'There will be a storm of protest from the newly elected [local] authorities in Wales if an assembly is to take their powers and reduce their influence within the Principality' (House of Lords, 3 July 1996). Conservatives want to shift more decision-taking to local institutions. That is where self-governing hospitals, and grant-maintained schools, come in. It is also the thinking behind our latest proposal to give more powers to parish councils. If people want to take more control over their own lives then they will respond more to the opportunity to contribute a local parish rate to pay for extra security on to their streets than to some remote regional assembly.

Openness and the Judge Over Your Shoulder

The Official Secrets Act of 1989 stripped away the criminal law from the great bulk of official information, so that economic forecasts, draft White Papers, correspondence dealing with decisions on individual benefits, etc., are no longer subject to an Official Secrets Act. John Major has done more to push forward open government than any of his predecessors. He has given the Ombudsman a new role in policing our code of access to government information. If any citizen wants to get information out of government and feels that a department is being unduly obstructive then he or she can complain via his or her MP to the Ombudsman, who can instruct the department to release the information.

The Citizen's Charter gives people much more information in dealing with the public sector than ever before and is transforming the ethos of the public services. It has the personal imprimatur of the Prime Minister, who was fed up with seeing the people who need public services the most being treated in a patronizing and offensive manner by petty bureaucrats. The Labour Party has always opposed our initiatives for giving out the practical information which people really want about the performance of their school or their hospital. Enabling people to compare the performance of different institutions raises questions about their performance which are too inconvenient for their friends and paymasters in the public-sector unions. If the entire Labour health team is financed by one of the health unions it is perhaps not surprising that they have not exactly been in the forefront of pressing for more information about individual hospitals. It is much more simple just to ask for more public money and never to confront the awkward truth that for any given amount of spending, some hospitals and schools do better than others.

Nowadays people expect openness from government and information about decisions affecting them. No longer will they just defer to the Great and the Good. And they want open codes of conduct for public officials and people in public life. We have a bold record of reform here. There is no significant area of extra information to which the Labour Party propose to give citizens access to which they do not have access at the moment. So what is the difference between Conservative and Labour? The answer is that Labour want to bring in the judges to interpret and enforce the provision which we have introduced. Putting, for example, our code of access to government information on a statutory footing would not necessarily give citizens any more actual information. The Australian Freedom of Information Act has fifteen sections containing 188 subsections listing the exemptions from its provisions. The exemptions in Mark Fisher's Bill here in 1993 needed fourteen sections with 108 subsections. This is a persistent theme in Labour's constitutional agenda. When it comes to freedom of information or a civil service code or the European Convention of Human Rights, they want more decisions to be taken by the judges. They would even have a new Bill of Rights, again to be interpreted by the judges – and who knows – perhaps its first test might be striking down Labour's plans for a windfall tax on the utilities as retrospective and discriminatory.

Labour never explain how judges themselves are going to remain unaffected by the new responsibilities which they wish to impose on them. Judges who were given a new role in enforcing a statutory Freedom of Information Act, or interpreting the European Convention on Human Rights (ECHR) would find themselves having to exercise enormous discretion. They would cease to be a neutral point outside the political system and would themselves become subject to political scrutiny in the way that judges have in America. Other countries with a different history have indeed given such power to their judges, but they have very different arrangements for the public scrutiny of judicial appointments and keeping the judiciary distinct from the legislature and the executive. It is absurd to imagine that one could somehow keep the established judicial arrangements of this country and yet also give British judges the enormous discretionary powers they enjoy in some other countries. It was striking for example how the press lavished attention on the Senate hearings on the appointment of Clarence Thomas to the Supreme Court of the United States of America while ignoring the simultaneous appointment of several senior judges to the supreme civil court here in Great Britain. If those judges were to be interpreting broad provisions of, for example, the ECHR we would all want (and be entitled) to know much more about their personal political beliefs.

The real problem for Labour is that they do not trust anyone to exercise discretion. The solution to this problem is apparently to turn to the judges who are supposed to possess an authority that the rest of us have lost. But why should judges manage any better, and why should their authority be preserved if they were brought into these difficult areas? The more one thinks about it the clearer it is that trying to put decisions in the hands of the judges is no solution at all.

Lords and Commons

We have seen that most of Labour's agenda is either irrelevant – they would not actually give citizens any more open access to information than they have already – or positively destructive by, for example, bringing the judiciary more into political debate and creating new tensions within the Union. But what is even more odd is that they do not have much to say about one of the most important parts of our political system where there is widely recognized to be a problem – the workings of the Commons itself. Here we have a good record of practical reform and there is more we can do.

Perhaps the most important recent reform has been the

introduction of departmentally related Select Committees, which have enormously enhanced the scope for backbench MPs to question and challenge the executive. Sometimes legislation comes before the House of Commons which is not as well drafted as it should be. We have responded to this problem by publishing more legislation in draft form so as to give time for interested parties and experts to comment even before the legislation is formally presented to the House of Commons. Now we are going yet further. For the first time the Queen's Speech in October 1996 announced not just our legislative proposals for the coming session but also draft legislation for the further year ahead. The Prime Minister has announced that he wants to move to a two-year rolling legislative programme, with the second year's proposals out in draft for consultation well in advance.

When we do legislate the legislation is often incomprehensible to the layman. One of Kenneth Clarke's most radical reforms has been to set in train the rewriting of our entire tax law, stage by stage, over the next five years so as to make it simpler and clearer.

Labour have not got much to say about the House of Commons. Their focus is the House of Lords. Yet again their muddled thinking would make the problem worse rather than better. They say that they want to reform the second chamber to remove the hereditary principle. They presumably look admiringly at the German Bundesrat or the American Senate. But a second democratically elected chamber could not function alongside the existing House of Commons without some over-arching structure which would enable potential conflicts between the two Houses to be resolved. The democratic superiority of the Commons enables our system to survive without establishing a new body or law superior to Parliament itself, which would mean a fundamental change to our constitution. Labour advanced halfway towards reform by announcing that they would abolish the hereditary peerage and then, faced with the dilemma of how a democratic second chamber could be rendered compatible with the House of Commons, have abandoned their quest. So instead we are only to have patronage peers appointed by the political parties. That is even worse than the current situation and has absolutely nothing to recommend it.

What Does This Tell Us About the Labour Party?

There is a belief running through Labour's programme that somehow Britain's constitutional arrangements are premodern, old-fashioned, out-of-touch, and that they need to be replaced with something much more Continental and up to date, so that we can once more look our French and German friends in the eye. Labour want to change us into a different sort of country – Bundesrepublik Britannien.

Conservatives simply ask: 'So what?' We have had a different history from the countries of the Continent and that does give our constitution a different shape from theirs. But that is not evidence that it is wrong. Different countries with their own traditions can quite reasonably have different constitutional arrangements. Tony Blair does not appear to be interested in the compatibility of his proposals with our long-established constitutional arrangements.

How have Labour got themselves into this mess? Above all it is because of their itch to intervene. The whole purpose of being a socialist is because you think you know how things should be organized. You set up a national plan to run the economy or you tear the heart out of our great cities and start again. Those particular ideas have gone out of fashion but Labour's instinct to intervene is as powerful as ever, so they have simply shifted their target. Now they want to do to our constitution what previously they did to our industry and our cities.

Back in 1934 Sir Stafford Cripps, the stern Fabian socialist, argued it was obvious that planning the economy was better than leaving it to the free market: after all, a 'body of competent engineers' could do it. That fatal conceit that politics was like engineering laid waste half the globe and nearly wrecked the British economy. But in their heart that is how Labour still think – only now it is the constitution which is to fall prey to that rationalist fallacy.

Conservatives do not claim that everything is perfect but we do understand what underpins our freedoms and our political stability in this country. No amount of ingenious legislation, no constitution however well designed, is of any use unless we enjoy what Michael Oakeshott called 'the political economy of freedom'. It is the rich and varied life of a civil society which best protects us:

Liberties, it is true, may be distinguished, and some may be more general or more settled and mature than others, but the freedom which the English libertarian knows and values lies in a coherence of mutually supporting liberties, each of which amplifies the whole and none of which stands alone. It springs neither from the separation of church and state, nor from the rule of law, nor from private property, nor from parliamentary government, nor from the write of *habeas corpus*, nor from the independence of the judiciary, nor from any one of the thousand other devices and arrangements characteristic of our society, but from what each signifies and represents, namely, the absence from our society of overwhelming concentration of power. This is the most general condition of our freedom, so general that all other conditions may be seen to be comprised within it . . .

That is why political refugees have fled to our country over the centuries, coming often from places with the most elaborate constitutional provisions on human rights, to one with no such written constitution. They knew where their freedoms were more secure.

NINE

Europe: Nation State or Federalism

Just about every issue which we have touched on so far re-emerges as a European issue too, and with an extra emotional charge because it ties in with our whole sense of our country's history, its independence and its role in the world. In the previous chapter, for example, we saw that Labour has a dangerous agenda for constitutional turmoil. But probably the biggest threat to our settled ways of governing ourselves comes from their European federalism. In Chapter 2 we saw the difference between enterprise and stakeholding economies and in Chapter 5 we saw how this particularly applied to the labour market. This resurfaces as a vivid argument about whether or not we should sign up for the Social Chapter as part of a European social model which Conservatives oppose and Labour support.

There is a deeper connection still between this chapter and the wider themes of the book. One of the arguments in the opening chapters was that the Conservative Party was the party of Middle England, deeply rooted in British common sense. We have always tried to protect Britain from the intellectual fads of elites harking after foreign models. New Labour has fallen for a new foreign model – Continental social democracy *circa* 1980. One of its last bastions is Brussels. Even as Continental governments gradually abandon it, the European Union remains a powerful device for pursuing that agenda. That is why one of the crucial distinguishing features of New Labour is European federalism. Because of all these concerns it is very easy for Conservatives to talk about what it is in Europe that we are against. But let us begin by looking at what we are for – our vision of Europe.

The Conservative Vision of Europe

Britain is an open trading nation with a rich and diverse network of international contacts. As Malcolm Rifkind has said:

8.6 million British citizens live overseas. Three in five of our people travel abroad each year . . . We export one quarter of all we produce; a greater share than Japan or the United States, more than Germany or France. We are the world's third largest outward investor: the biggest foreign investor in the US; the third largest source of private capital to the developing world. Last year our total assets abroad exceeded £1.4 trillion. We had a net income of over £10 billion from our investments overseas. (Malcolm Rifkind, Chatham House, 21 September 1995)

If travel and commerce bring people together then that is very welcome. The Treaty of Rome calls for 'an ever closer union among the peoples of Europe' not among the states of Europe.

The European Community began as an instrument of Franco-German reconciliation after the Second World War. That it is now the pre-eminent European political institution is a genuine and legitimate source of pride to both countries. But their very achievement in creating an institution which has performed rather better during the post-war period than the ones to which we pinned our hopes, such as Efta (the European Free Trade Area) or the Commonwealth, has itself now become a problem. We do not want a small and exclusive Europe of Charlemagne. By contrast, our vision of Europe is big, inclusive, and tolerant of diversity.

One of our highest priorities is European enlargement. To prepare for enlargement we need to do as much as possible to open up the single market to access for goods and services from would-be members of the European Union. There is nothing more depressing than visiting one of the capitals of the newly liberated countries of Central Europe and hearing from members of their Governments that all they want to do is sell us their beetroot or their bacon without having to face hostile tariffs. If they could do that now they would perhaps be in better economic shape to join us in a few years' time. Europe can take no pride in the remaining trade barriers to future members on our eastern border.

A larger Europe must inevitably be flexible – what is some-times called a Europe of 'variable geometry'. Malcolm Rifkind, the Foreign Secretary, has outlined our approach here:

First, such flexibility must not undermine the core of disciplines and obligations on which the single market depends. Secondly, no member state should be excluded from an area of policy in which it is qualified and it wishes to participate – policies must be open to all. Thirdly, there should be no inner and outer circles – no two-tier Europe . . . A further principle with regard to flexibility . . . is that policies using Community institutions and the Community budget should be undertaken by less than the full membership only when that is agreed by all. Policies agreed by some against the objections of others should not carry the imprimatur of the European Union, or use EU institutions or resources. (*Hansard*, 21 March 1996, cols. 517–18)

The European Union can give the impression that the only way in which it can define a European identity is by knowing what it is against. Being anti-American in foreign and defence matters and anti-Japanese in industrial and economic matters is not a secure base for European cooperation. We must keep our strong links with America, particularly military cooperation in Nato, and similarly we can welcome Japanese industrial investment. Europe's great history and culture should themselves provide us with a secure enough sense of identity.

We need to push forward the internal-market programme which was first launched by Margaret Thatcher and Lord Cockfield in 1985, recognizing exactly what the single market means. It is not quite the same as classic nineteenth-century free trade – it goes much further than that. For a start, if a product or service or academic qualification meets the requirements of any member state of the European Union then it must be acceptable everywhere else in the European Union. This goes beyond traditional free trade, in which foreign goods can be sold in one's own country provided they meet one's domestic regulatory requirements. Now they can be sold in our country if they meet another EU member's regulatory requirements. This is mutual recognition.

The second distinctive feature of the single market is a supranational authority in the European Commission and the Court of Justice to act as prosecutor and judge to enforce open markets. If the French Government tries to stop a British firm from exporting to France, then that firm can apply to the European Commission for fair treatment from the French. One of the most dramatic examples of this policy is in government aid to industry. No individual national Government is going to police its own aid; instead, they can police each other within the EC by mutual jealousy – a much more effective discipline. The Commission then requires individual nation states to recover subsidies which it considers to be a distortion of the market. Not all member states are yet abiding by the letter, let alone the spirit, of the single market. Britain as a great trading nation has a particular interest in pushing this forward and we can use the disciplines of the European Union to our advantage. British Airways, for example was able to use the single-market rules finally to get access to Orly Airport and hence internal French connecting flights. There are many other such battles to be fought, particularly in areas such as financial services, where countries which have a federalist rhetoric in theory seem peculiarly slow to implement even modest opening of markets in practice.

The European Court of Justice (ECJ) too often appears to work to an agenda of European federalism which British Conservatives simply cannot accept. We have suggested as part of the Intergovernmental Conference limiting the retrospective application of its judgments, which can cause havoc to businessmen and others, and also an internal appeals procedure. We also would like to see streamlined procedures for the rapid amendment of European legislation that has been interpreted by the ECJ in a way never intended by the Council.

Subsidiarity is another important theme of our approach to Europe. We welcome the approach of Jacques Santer, who believes in 'less but better'. The amount of European legislation has fallen from sixty-one draft directives in 1990 to nineteen in 1996. This is much better than trying to intervene in the 'nooks and crannies of national life' as Douglas Hurd warned. We are seeking a treaty provision clarifying the application of subsidiarity in the interpretation of European law.

All this adds up to a substantial agenda for the future. It is not the approach of a party of Little Englanders. We have an attractive, constructive vision of a new enlarged European Union which takes fully into account the diversity of its peoples, cultures and traditions. We are taking the lead on enlargement, reform of the CAP, anti-fraud measures, deregulation, putting the budget on a sounder footing, and subsidiarity.

The European Social Model

Europe's historic strength has been its diversity. No single power in modern times has succeeded in controlling all of Europe. If the prince did not like the ideas you were publishing or the scientific experiments you were conducting, you could always flee across the border to another country where you would be tolerated. Europe is a continuous experiment in which different social and economic arrangements can be compared.

We have now learned from the environmentalists that the world needs a rich and varied genetic bank in order to survive. It is good to have different breeds of plants and animals so that even if one falls prey to a new virus or a change in taste, others can come in to fill the gap. And just as we need biodiversity so we also need political and economic diversity. This is relevant to the argument which we studied in Chapters 4 and 5 between free marketeers and stakeholders. Stakeholding is a fashionable word for the old-fashioned social democratic Continental model. British free marketeers believe that it is unable to deliver either full employment or social cohesion. But there is a crucial difference between the two sides of the argument. Genuine free marketeers want to enable a diversity of corporate cultures to flourish: if an individual company wishes to be a stakeholder company, so be it. Our market changes have made that more possible. BT now calls itself a stakeholder company: one of the many benefits of privatization. Indeed, our liberal regime can make it easier for stakeholder companies to flourish than it is on the Continent. There was a fascinating letter in the *Financial Times* of 7 February 1996 from Robert Bischof, the chairman of the Boss group. He defended the German model of corporate governance but went on at the end of his letter to make the following remarks:

The problem with Germany's system is not its basic principle but that it has been perverted by a mass of legal and institutional red tape. It is also true that it has led some German management boards to be too preoccupied with seeking consensus and with pursuing long-term strategies, where tough decisions were needed . . .

In Boss, like in most continental and Japanese-owned companies, we have of course the best of both worlds: we practise our stakeholder culture and are not restricted by the paraphernalia of an institutionalized framework. Hence it's such a joy to run companies in Britain.

Believers in the European social model want to use the Social Chapter to force uniformity on everyone. They talk of a 'level playing field' as if we are creating a Europe of which the most fastidious groundsman could be proud. But open competition does not require that the teams be identical – they can be coached differently and play differently. Tony Blair tried to avoid confronting the threat from the Social Chapter to which he is committed when he spoke at the CBI conference in November 1995. He said:

The Social Chapter is not detailed legislation. It is a set of principles ... Each piece of legislation will be judged on its merits. I have no intention whatever of agreeing to anything and everything that emerges from the EU. Proposals are just that: proposals. And they will be examined, with you, on their merits.

He was either extraordinarily ill-informed or deliberately misleading his audience. He had to be corrected by the Director-General of the CBI, Adair Turner:

Let me finish with a comment on Tony Blair's suggestion at our conference that a Labour Party might pick and choose which directives under the Social Chapter it wished to put into place in the UK. If you sign up to the Social Chapter you cannot actually be sure that you will have your way because some directives will be covered by qualified majority voting. There is however a way to pick and choose and that is available to the Labour Party if it wants to have it as its policy. The way to pick and choose is actually not to sign up to the Social Chapter. (Adair Turner, 2 December 1995)

European Monetary Union

John Major used his formidable negotiating skills at Maastricht to secure for us an opt-out from Stage Three of European Monetary Union. He has ensured that the United Kingdom will decide on whether it would be in the national interest to join a single currency should that possibility arise. At the moment we do not know for certain whether a single currency will go ahead, and if so, when it will go ahead and which countries would be eligible to participate in it anyway.

All the implications of EMU would need to be very carefully considered. Many Conservatives see great difficulties in it. The Prime Minister has made it clear that if there were a decision to join a single currency it would have to be put to the electorate in a referendum because it would be one of the most important economic and political choices made by a British government in decades. Labour see it as simply a matter of ensuring that the right economic conditions are created before entry. As Mr Blair has said:

First the key question is whether we can, through greater cooperation, achieve the degree of integration and convergence necessary for a single currency . . . and how we persuade the people of Europe that this is a step that it is sensible and right to take. (Tony Blair, Brussels, 10 January 1995)

Britain Isolated: Continent Cut Off?

Britain often appears to be the odd man out in Europe. There are times when Britain's approach to issues differs from that of many of its partners. There are several reasons for this. One is that Britain is particularly scrupulous in meeting our Community obligations and as a result, we tend to think rather more rigorously than some other member states about what it is that we are being asked to sign up to. Between 1990 and 1994, for example, only six cases against the UK were referred to the European Court of Justice compared with an average of thirty for other member states. Only Denmark (with four cases referred) did better.

Secondly, we have a long and stable political history and a constitution with which we are comfortable like an old suit. As the mechanism whereby a new Europe is to be created often appears to be political and constitutional change, it means that price is one which comes particularly high for Great Britain. If your country has been invaded and reconstructed several times during this century your constitutional arrangements are less tied up with your sense of national identity than ours.

Thirdly, we have successfully modernized our economy during the period since 1979. The single market aside, the European Community often appears more as an obstacle than an encouragement to this process. By contrast on the Continent, particularly the south, the European Community is seen as an important agent for modernization as it is so closely tied in with the Continent's recovery after the Second World War.

For these reasons it often feels as if Britain is fighting on its own in European negotiations. (Actually things look rather different on the Continent – where the single market is sometimes seen as a plot to impose Anglo-American capitalism on traditional corporatist societies.) Nevertheless there is something in this picture. It can give rise to two very different types of defeatism.

The first type of defeatism is to say that the only thing to do is leave. A more dishonest version of that is to suggest that somehow we can fundamentally renegotiate the terms of membership so that we are both members but do not have to accept the obligations which come with membership. The Prime Minister has bluntly rejected this line of argument:

We are in Europe and we all know we are staying in Europe . . . Some suggest we could just negotiate a trading relationship with Europe. But frankly, the idea that if we are outside the EU we could somehow become a trading haven on the edge of Europe with all the benefits of that vital market of 370 million – while others fixed the rules without any regard at all to our national self-interest – is cloud-cuckoo land. (John Major, Institute of Directors, 24 April 1996)

Several European countries have tried precisely that approach – not being members of the European Union but linked to it in a free-trade European economic area. But they ended applying for full membership because they found that this peripheral status gave them the worst of all possible worlds – they could sell their goods into the single market but only if they met all the rules of the single market, which were decided at meetings where they were not represented.

There is a second sort of defeatism which is to say that it is so embarrassing that sometimes Britain has to exercise our veto that we should stop doing so and just give in. This is Tony Blair's approach – 'Under my leadership, I will never allow this country to be isolated or left behind in Europe' (Tony Blair,

Blackpool, 4 October 1994). Labour explicitly say that they reject 'permanent opt-outs or variable geometry' and that they will give up our veto in some areas of European decision-taking. Not only would this do us great economic harm, it would also create massive political, indeed constitutional, upheaval. To extend the areas where a British Parliament and a British Government could be overruled in Brussels would not be acceptable to the British people. On its own this is reason enough not to vote Labour at the next election.

III POLITICS

TEN

Hot Politics and Cool Politics

We have all seen it on the television: campaigners who are passionate, committed, articulate ranged against the Minister who sounds wary, cautious, perhaps even downright negative. The campaigners are after something clear and straightforward and they are marshalling the arguments to force the Government to do it. We know the issues and the personal tragedies which make them vivid: a parent whose child has died in the crash of a school coach demanding that seat-belts on them be compulsory; someone who has contracted HIV or hepatitis from an infected blood transfusion who wants compensation from the NHS; a protester standing in a beautiful field threatened by a bypass; somebody who has given up their time for a good cause and cannot understand why virtuous activities should have to pay VAT just like vicious ones; the victim of a financial fraud asking for compensation; a well-respected officer in the armed services forced to leave because he is gay.

These individual campaigners are engaged in what Marshall McLuhan called 'hot politics'. It is direct, emotional and personal. It engages our sympathies and our attention. Thinking about the wider implications seems almost to insult the people who are suffering some personal tragedy. And what of the Minister? He is on a different wavelength. He is talking 'cool politics' and it does not have the same impact. The viewer is left thinking he should give in to whatever the demand may be and show for once that the Government will respond to what the people want. If you are a Conservative, you probably thought when you saw such a scene on the TV: 'Why can't those ministers get out from behind their Whitehall desks and be more political?' If you are not a Conservative you are likely to have thought that it was just typical of this Government that we could not concede to the wishes of people who are clearly so much more passionate and committed.

If there is an Opposition spokesman on the programme he will have shown just that extra bit of sympathy, that extra inclination to go a bit further in meeting the group's demands. It will not necessarily be explicit but over the years they have mastered the art of the nudge, the nod, the hint that somehow things would be different and better if they were in office. Often they do not need to do anything so rash as actually to give an explicit pledge of spending money or passing the requisite legislation – a demand for an 'independent inquiry' will do. But the tone is clear – 'we understand, we will look after you'.

We experience it week after week. The broadcasters, who see it as just doing their job, choose the most articulate and presentable advocates of any case so that they can put the Minister on the spot. The representatives from Labour or the Liberal Democrats just coast along in the wake of the campaigners, showing that at least their hearts have not been frozen by years of high office.

More and more people feel that real politics is hot. So they join pressure groups that campaign on one particular cause. It might be the Greens, a Nationalist party, animal rights, a local campaign to 'save' a hospital or a school or stop a bypass. These campaigns feed off a wider temperamental shift towards immediate emotional engagement and benevolence which often now seems to be the only moral and authentic position. Edmund Burke, needless to say, identified the danger of this as vividly as anyone:

... I have observed that the philosophers, in order to insinuate their polluted atheism into young minds, systematically flatter all their passions, natural and unnatural. They explode, or render odious or contemptible, that class of virtues which restrain the appetite . . . In place of all this, they substitute a virtue which they call humanity or benevolence. By these means their morality has no idea in it of restraint, or indeed of a distinct set of principles of any kind. When their disciples are thus left free, and guided only by present feeling, they are no longer to be depended upon for good or evil. The men who, today, snatch the worst criminals from justice, will murder the most innocent persons tomorrow.

The trouble with these 'hot' politicians is that they do not have to take responsibility for the long term. Indeed, some of the Government's worst mistakes have come from acceding to these short-term demands without regard to the longer-term consequences. Some of the newspapers that criticize the Dangerous Dogs Act and run sympathetic profiles of some ageing bull terrier on 'death row' are the very same ones which a few years ago were putting on their front pages horrible photographs of children savaged by a neighbour's dog. Eventually the pressures on the Government to do something were irresistible but policy-making in response to that sort of hot campaigning rarely stands up in the long term.

Sometimes the consequences can be perverse. If you have suffered as a result of fraud perpetrated by a financial institution to which you entrusted your savings and you successfully get compensation from the Government, then the message to everyone else is clear. They can relax. They do not need to worry about whether the absurdly high returns being advertised are genuine because they will always be bailed out by the taxpayer.

Sometimes the campaigners seem to think they should be immune from the usual disciplines of scientific and economic appraisal within which government inevitably has to work. The successful Greenpeace campaign against the sinking of the Brent Spar oil rig was an outrageous example of this: the campaigners hoodwinked the media in a way which no Government could or should ever have got away with. That demonstration of political power may have marked a turning-point. These organizations are well-financed and skilled manipulators of public opinion. The media has treated them with the sort of deference which Ministers enjoyed forty years ago. But now their power is such that they must face the same scrutiny and challenge as Ministers and then their more lurid claims will be revealed for what they are.

Commentators, Spin Doctors, and the Spiral of Silence

We have seen how the responsibilities of being a national governing party can lead Ministers to seem cool and distant compared with the passions of hot politics. There is a second phenomenon which can also appear to distance politicians even when they wish directly to engage with people – the rise of the commentator.

Imagine that it is the Second World War and the family is huddled around the wireless listening to one of Churchill's wartime speeches, but it is being broadcast in the modern style. After the first few minutes Churchill's voice is faded out and instead three rival commentators start explaining the significance of what they think Churchill is saying. One claims that he is really trying to placate Conservatives unhappy with lack of progress. Another says that the words have been carefully chosen to appeal to Roosevelt and get the Americans into the war. A third says that Churchill's interpretation of the latest news from North Africa is too optimistic. And all three talk with great confidence about Churchill's motives – which are seen as essentially crude and manipulative.

It is one of the paradoxes of modern broadcasting technology that whereas it has the potential to bring us much more directly in contact with political events, it all too often serves to distance us, interposing an interpreter between us and the real action. It cools down our response to the politician and sets him at a great distance. (The rise of the spin doctor incidentally is a response to the rise of the commentator.)

Imagine you hear a Minister saying something which sounds quite sensible or strikes a chord with you but immediately afterwards the commentators analyse it to pieces. This leaves you unsure about your own reaction. Can you trust your own instincts – perhaps not? The broadcasters say it is just a useful corrective, some professional scepticism. But they can take it too far and now we have evidence of this. If you ask people about their own experience of, say, the NHS, they are likely to rate it very highly. But if you then ask them what they think of the state of the NHS in general they are likely to give a much less favourable response. The same goes for a wide range of public issues. It is even true of voters' assessment of MPs: ask what people think of MPs in general and we get a very low rating indeed. Ask them what they think of their own MP and he or she will do rather better.

There is a similar phenomenon with voting intentions – the 'spiral of silence'. The most systematic study of this phenomenon (Sparrow and Turner, 'Messages from the spiral of silence', *Journal of the Market Research Society*, vol. 37, no. 4), puts it like this:

Research has indicated that individuals will refrain from expressing their perceived minority views in the face of a hostile climate of opinion . . . The true position on issues is obscured by the inclination of a large group of Conservative voters to refrain from nominating their party on any issue against what they see as a hostile climate of opinion.

This helps to explain the notorious failure of the opinion pollsters successfully to predict voting in the 1992 general election. There was not just a dramatic late swing to us. It also looks as if Conservative support was systematically underestimated throughout the campaign. A lot of Conservative voters reported themselves as uncertain as to whether they would vote or as don't knows because they felt that the media climate was hostile to Conservatives. That reinforces the perception that the world is anti-Conservative and leads even more Conservative-inclined supporters to stay even more quiet – and so the spiral of silence is created. There are many Conservatives out there trapped in such a spiral: now is the time to break out of it.

National Politics

The Conservative Party has a distinctive strength as *the* national party which understands best how to reconcile the potent demands of hot politics with our need to rub along together on these islands.

One of the reasons for the strong dramatic appeal made by individual campaigners is they do not have to think about how their demands can be reconciled with anyone else's. The very force of the demand, for example, to ban all handguns or ban fox hunting, comes from its narrow focus. The campaigners do not have to think about what this means for Olympic sportsmen and women, or people in rural areas where hunting is part of their traditional way of life. It falls to Government to work out how these different demands should be balanced and reconciled. That is what national Government is about and it is more serious and more difficult than campaigning on particular issues.

Liberal Democrats have long seen politics as simply a matter of appealing to each individual interest group. They have been doing this for over 100 years. Gladstone's 1892 Newcastle programme was denounced at the time as a charter for 'faddists'. Their lack of a clear, nationwide identity enables them to run a range of wholly incompatible local campaigns. As for socialism, Orwell famously observed that it always seemed to attract sandal-wearing naturists. New Labour is more shameless than ever in pandering to every interest group. But it is not just that Labour now plays the game of interest-group politics like the Liberal Democrats. There is a deeper and more fundamental problem. If you believe in big government with regulation, intervention and public spending in its armoury, then you feed the appetites of the interest groups. They fight to get favours out of Government knowing there is a prize to be gained. A Hobbesian battle of all against all is fought out over the terrain of big government.

Winston Churchill objected to protectionism because he said

it would lead to the 'Americanisation of British politics'. By that he meant that if the Government was passing lots of detailed laws fixing tariffs or banning particular imports, then the House of Commons would descend into pork-barrel politics. The more that Government claims to be able to do then the greater the risk that interest groups will try to capture it to use it for their own purposes. The shift from the corrupt patronage politics of the eighteenth century to the higher moral tone of the Victorian period was achieved by rolling back Government. Free trade and limited Government are the best guarantee of high standards in politics.

ELEVEN

New Labour, New Danger

Old Labour, New Labour

One of the rhetorical devices of a Blair speech is to attack the 'New Right' and 'Old Labour' and then with a sort of linguistic inevitability to offer 'New Labour' instead. We have already seen, particularly in Chapters 1–3, that the 'New Right' is not quite as it is portrayed by Labour. Indeed Labour's tendency to caricature the free market as morally unacceptable selfishness run riot shows how little they understand the reality of a free-market economy.

Labour leaders have long recognized that just about the most politically unpopular cause in the country is left-wing socialism. They do not see why they should just leave the Conservative Party to attack the Left – they like to join in too. Neil Kinnock came closest to gaining the respect of the electorate when he attacked militant Labour councillors in Liverpool. It always plays well with the media because Conservatives attacking left-wing socialism is really rather obvious but for Labour leaders to do it is still a story. Indeed one sometimes suspects that attacking their own left-wing has always been the Labour leadership's main political weapon in difficult times (in the 1930s and 1940s losing the Whip became a rite of passage for any serious left-wing politician).

It is obvious that Blair's Labour Party is not Michael Foot's Labour Party. But that is not the end of the matter. It is the starting-point for a critique of New Labour. The argument is not now about whether Labour has changed; it is about what Labour has changed into. 'Change' is perhaps not the right word. 'Transmute' is more accurate. Those long-standing Labour instincts to back trade unions, intervene in industry, spend more and raise taxes, are still as potent as ever, but they are expressed in a different way.

The Labour Party was formed as the electoral vehicle of the trade-union movement and the links remain strong. Tony Blair claims that they do not want to return to the days of unballoted strikes. But their new language of 'stakeholding' takes us back to the Labour Left's campaign for 'industrial democracy'. It offers a new rationale for aggressive trade unionism. They have backed up this rhetoric with specific pledges to make it an offence for an employer to refuse to recognize a trade union or to sack a striker – new legal privileges greater than those which unions enjoyed in the 1970s.

Labour no longer intend to nationalize the twenty-five leading companies or to impose planning agreements on them. But they do have a programme for detailed intervention in their affairs through new regulations, the European Social Chapter and the statutory minimum wage – which was explicitly considered and rejected by the Wilson Government in the 1970s. In the past they threatened the national interest by unilateral disarmament and pulling out of Europe altogether. Now they are willing to surrender more power to Brussels, giving up the national veto in 'social, environmental, industrial, and regional policy' to quote Tony Blair's own words.

When it comes to the constitution one is reminded of the observation that the Bourbons after the French Revolution had 'learnt nothing and forgotten nothing'. Blair wants to pick up exactly where Callaghan left off in 1979 with the massive and intricate legislation on devolution which brought the last Labour Government down.

If 'New Labour' ever get into power, they would have to put up taxes to pay for the eighty-nine spending pledges made by Tony Blair and his leading spokesmen or contained in the draft manifesto which the party has endorsed. Labour would have to put up taxes such as business rates and income tax to raise some of the revenue in the same old way. But what makes 'New Labour' so dangerous is that they have devised new taxes that would be introduced by the back door – a new levy here, an upwards review there. They hope that these new taxes would raise the revenue they would need – without the electoral consequences of their old methods.

'New Labour' will pretend that their new taxes are not taxes at all. But the result would be every bit as damaging as any increase in direct taxation. Whatever they call them, however they collect them, it is Labour's way of taking money to pay for higher public spending. Blair claims to have learned the lessons of Labour's past and that there will be no more tax-and-spend socialism. But Labour have accumulated a series of commitments to new taxes or quasi-taxes which belie his assurances. The ten most egregious examples are:

- *a new teenage tax* – Labour would abolish child benefit for sixteen–eighteen-year-olds who stay on at school;
- *a new utilities tax* – Labour would introduce a windfall tax on the privatized utilities;
- *a new Tartan tax* – although Labour would now call a referendum on their proposals for a Scottish Parliament, it is clear that they would still prefer such a body to be endowed with tax-raising powers;
- *a new London tax* – Labour's new authority for London would have 'limited spending and tax-raising powers';
- *a new graduate tax* – Labour would replace the current system of student grants and loans with an extended system of repayment through the National Insurance system;
- *a new higher council tax* – Labour have a 'restated commitment to dropping capping';
- *a new private-health tax* – Labour would remove reliefs on private medical insurance, currently available to those aged sixty or over:

- *a new telephone tax* – Labour's spokesman on information technology, Geoff Hoon MP, has said, 'There will be a levy on consumers to meet the costs of connecting every school to the information superhighway';
- *a new inheritance tax* – Labour would reduce or abolish reliefs on inheritance tax;
- *a new training tax* – Labour would force employers to provide specified levels of training. Those who do not meet Labour's standards would be subject to a compulsory levy.

From this list one can see that Labour have learned the lesson that tax increases and spending pledges need to be disguised rather better than they were in the past. But whatever the ingenious formula which they use, the reality of the increase in the burden on families and firms is just the same.

Paradoxes of the Project

'Community', 'globalization', 'insecurity', 'short-termism', 'stakeholder', 'centralization', 'constitutional reform', 'Americanization', 'social inclusion'. These are the buzzwords of New Labour's political economy, which the author analysed in *Blair's Gurus* (Centre for Policy Studies, 1996). One is reminded of George Orwell's strictures on politicians' prose:

As soon as certain topics are raised, the concrete melts into the abstract and no one seems able to think of terms of speech that are not hackneyed: prose consists less and less of words chosen for the sake of their meaning and more and more of phrases tacked together like the sections of a prefabricated hen-house.

What lies behind the buzzwords? The clue is what Labour insiders call 'The Project'. The Project is first and foremost to modernize the Labour Party. They want to break free from the old doctrines of command-economy socialism. Their model has clearly been Continental social democracy, notably the German Social Democrats. There is a striking parallel between the decision by the German Social Democrats in 1959 at Bad

Godesberg explicitly to renounce command-economy socialism and Tony Blair's campaign to rewrite Clause 4. 'Social Democracy' must look like an appealing alternative to 'socialism' after the excesses of the Labour Party in the 1970s and 1980s: no wonder these two expressions can still prompt rancorous arguments inside the Labour Party.

Another model is Clinton's 'New Democrats'. Labour have certainly turned to them for lessons in political tactics but the buzzwords identified earlier hardly add up to a passionate endorsement of American values. Rather what Blair shares with some of Clinton's advisers is a dislike of what they dismissively term 'Anglo-American capitalism'. The East Coast intellectuals who helped shape Clintonomics look enviously at German and Japanese industrial and social policies. So even Labour's ties to New Democrats in America lead back eventually to Continental social democracy.

Embracing Continental social democracy looks like a bold break with traditional socialism. But Labour have been trapped by the models they have followed. They have finally caught up with Continental social democracy just at the point when it itself is now in crisis. The Left in France and in Spain are in total disarray. Social democrats in Germany have not won an election since 1976. Perhaps only in Italy is there some hope for Labour and there the separatist forces unleashed by the collapse of the old political system are already putting massive pressures on the new one. And all across the Continent they look enviously at the success of Britain and the USA in delivering more jobs and encouraging new investment. Perhaps fifteen years ago for Labour to have adopted Continental social democracy would have put it abreast of events. Now it is still struggling to catch up. Here we get to the crucial paradox of Blair's project: their model for modernizing the party is not one for modernizing the country.

What About Labour Governing?

Back in the summer of 1996 Labour launched their *Road to the Manifesto* and proudly identified their five priority pledges for government. These were commitments to, for example, abolish the Assisted Places Scheme and save money with unspecified changes in the management structure of the NHS. Soon the details unravelled as it became clear that Labour had not, for example, included the extra cost of educating children in the state system rather than through the Assisted Places Scheme. It is not just that their figures did not add up. Labour supporters in the media and elsewhere said gleefully after the launch of the document that this proved that there was nothing to worry about from a Labour Government because it would do nothing. They looked forward to it as if Blair's team would be like Whig grandees keeping the ship of state afloat and uttering vaguely progressive sentiments but not doing much in particular.

But this is a comforting illusion as one can see as soon as one considers what would happen if Tony Blair became Prime Minister. The best way of judging a Blair Government is to think where its energies would be absorbed. It is clear that between them four areas of policy would absorb the time and commitment of any Blair Government.

First, the legislative programme would be dominated by constitutional issues. They would need a Bill to hold referendums in Scotland and Wales. Even if there were a clear result from the referendum in favour of devolution in principle there would still be a host of tricky practical issues to sort out in detailed legislation. There are already signs from the Labour Whips that they would like to take the devolution measures out of the Chamber of the House and upstairs into committee, because they are aware of how much damage the last Labour Government suffered when it got bogged down in devolution legislation. But it is a clear rule of the House of Commons that constitutional measures all have to be debated entirely on the floor of the House of Commons. This is our way, in a

Parliamentary system without a written constitution, of giving special protection to our constitutional rights. The rule reflects the point that changing the constitutional structure is not quite the same as changing tax rates or selling off a nationalized industry. It would be impossible for a Labour Government both to claim that they are trying to strengthen our constitution and at the same time remove one of our clearest and most long-established constitutional protections. So Labour would have to expect that for at least the first two years they were in office legislation on devolution would take up a huge part of Parliament's time.

For the rest of the time they would be bogged down in implementing their windfall taxes on the privatized utilities. Labour seem to imagine that it could be introduced in a Budget immediately after the election but again it is much more complicated than that. They expect to raise £5–£10 billion but they have not been willing to answer the simple question as to which companies would pay the tax. This may be because they realize that it is fraught with difficulty. To raise the money necessary to pay the tax the utilities would have to put up their prices. Since privatization, and even after VAT, the real price of electricity has fallen by 5 per cent and of gas by 8 per cent. If the cost of the windfall tax were passed on to consumers they could find themselves paying much higher prices which would more than wipe out these gains. If this were not allowed then, instead, investment would suffer and shareholders would see a big reduction in the value of their shares. And those shares belong to you and me – either directly or through our pension schemes. However Labour do it, a windfall tax eventually hits us either through price increases or through reductions in the value of our savings. The businesses would fight back through the British courts, challenging the unfairness of the proposal which discriminates between different firms and is five years retrospective. No longer should Labour presume that this process would stop at the British courts. The European courts could well have a view on it too. And we already know that the American companies which might be hit by the tax have urged the Clinton Administration to take retaliatory action against British firms. Getting the windfall tax through would take up the energies of Labour's Treasury team for years. And all it would achieve would be to damage vital and competitive British industries – what a waste of effort.

The third challenge facing them would be to head off the pressure from public-sector unions for higher pay. Looking around the ranks of New Labour one thing is clear above all – they represent the public sector. Many of their candidates and MPs have worked in the public sector. Others are councillors who cheered most loudly that part of Tony Blair's speech at his last party conference in which he promised to end rate capping so they could put up their council tax. The interest groups whose influence we studied in the previous chapter all expect Labour to look after them with higher public spending. And specific Labour policies such as the minimum wage come with a clear spending cost. Meeting these public spending pressures will be the other main task of any incoming Labour Treasury team.

Fourthly, the intergovernmental conference on the future of the European Union will be coming to its conclusion. As part of his announced policy of 'never being isolated in Europe' Tony Blair will wish to abandon the British Government's veto in important areas and shift further powers towards Brussels. It will then need a major piece of legislation to implement these changes, legislation which would be opposed not only by Conservative MPs but by some on his own side.

There is one thing that all these four measures have in common. They do absolutely nothing to address the everyday concerns of the British citizen. They do not create an extra job or make us safer on the streets. So Labour would be expending a massive amount of political energy not to meet the concerns of the voter but to take them further away from the ordinary voter. It is why Labour have never in their history managed to deliver two successive majority governments that go anything like their full term. Their beliefs and their agenda are so out of touch with the views of Middle England that they soon lose support and collapse. It would be far better if we did not have to learn that painful lesson over again.

There is an underlying left-wing taste for radical reconstruction of our country which has wrought more havoc than any other economic or social movement. In the post-war period we have seen it applied to the physical reconstruction of our towns, to a belief in fundamental economic planning, and now, as we saw in Chapter 8, it is to be applied to the British Constitution (and to the constitution of our companies). It was left-wing visionaries who said of the manufacturing towns of the North and the Midlands that it would be 'beneficial to raze potentially everything and start all over again'. That is why our cities now look as if they were heavily bombed even if they were not. And they destroyed many great schools with their forced march to comprehensives and uniformity no matter what the cost. That same left-wing urge for fundamental reconstruction is still there, it is just that the labels are different. Now it is our constitution which is to be vandalized and the legal framework of our companies which is to be transformed. Blair's Labour Party has successfully defeated the old entryists of the Militant Tendency. But they have been taken over by a new set of entryists – constitutional militants – who want to transform the way we are governed, and a federalist tendency who are happy to hand over our powers of self-government to Brussels. At the very moment they were defeating the Socialist Workers Party, Charter 88 was taking over the Labour Party.

That itch to transform us is what distinguishes parties of the Left from the Conservative Party. It shows in Tony Blair's bizarre claim that Britain is a 'young country' as if he is after some sort of Year Zero in the style of the French Revolution. But we are not a young country. We are an old country with a great future, and indeed one whose future depends on appreciating and learning from its past, as we shall see in the final chapter.

TWELVE

The Conservative Opportunity

Who Do We Think We Are?

British Conservatism draws its strength from a kind of forward-looking memory. We have a picture of our country and its history which helps shape our policies for the future. We see ourselves as a nation of traders and developers, entrepreneurs and speculators, freebooters and buccaneers. London's clubs and coffee houses turned into what was the world's insurance market: so much for the belief that there is some new and dangerous process by which markets subvert ancient social institutions. A recent history of eighteenth-century England draws its title from Blackstone's description of us as a 'polite and commercial people': it is not a bad picture to have of ourselves. That historical vision then guides us into the future as enterprising, flexible, vigorous, free marketeers.

Labour have a vision of our country too. They are not fighting the coming election just for fun. We should do them the credit of taking Blair's high-flown rhetoric seriously. They want to modernize our country and their model is rather different from ours. For them as we have already seen, it is constitutional and economic changes to make us fit the model of Continental social democracy *circa* 1980. The contrast between these two models is most vivid – and most measurable – in economic management. There the evidence of British success is piling up so as to be absolutely compelling. Labour have therefore tried to reverse

President Clinton's campaign adage: for them it is – 'Keep it off the economy, stupid'. They know that if the election is fought on our economic prospects they will lose.

The Enterprise Centre of Europe

Labour's Continental economic model would never work for us. It is not true to our history and our traditions. We are too individualist ever to be able to allow our economy to be run through deals by the 'social partners'. But it did once work for Germany, Austria, and to some extent France. Now the boot is on the other foot. They are increasingly recognizing that their model is no longer working. The President of the German CBI contrasted our recent economic success with their problems in the following terms: 'We have too rigid labour laws. We have too high social costs and taxes. We have the shortest working week in Europe . . . No wonder we have a problem' (*Daily Telegraph*, 17 January 1996).

It is that Continental model which looks as if it will not survive into the twenty-first century, as it is so ill-suited for the new global economy. We are in the opposite situation. Our experience of the first Industrial Revolution did not prepare us well for mass manufacturing in a mature industrial society. But now we are coming back into our own. There is no need for us to succumb to the Europe-envy which so pervades the politics of Tony Blair and his followers. We are well placed for the challenges of the twenty-first century. We have already slain formidable dragons such as trade-union power and chronic inflation but we cannot rest on our laurels. The world does not stop. We are in better shape but the world is a tougher place. It is not just a matter of the Asian tigers: most of the world is now rejoining the open trading system and some will be formidable competitors. What we now have to do is to apply to these new challenges the same guts and determination that we displayed in taking on the challenges of the 1970s and 1980s. What are these advantages which we can take into the new global economy and how can we best exploit them for the benefit of all our people?

Our language is not just a thing of beauty: it is also an extraordinary commercial asset. This may seem far removed from the world of technology, but actually much of today's value lies in the software not the hardware and this has always been an area where Britain excels. It is law and accountancy, but it is advertising and pop lyrics too. Eighty-five per cent of the world's computer software is written in English.

The industry which transmits all this software is, in its broadest sense, telecommunications, and here again we are now very strong because of a combination of our language and our global outlook. More international phone calls are made from London than from any other city in the world. After opening up our domestic telephone market we are now going to open up our entire international phone traffic to anyone who wants to run international calls in and out of the UK. In the words of Hamish Macrae, 'Expect this particular bit of deregulation to be seen, in twenty years' time, as the most important single economic decision this Government has made. We are gaining a central role in creating the high-tech infrastructure for the next century' (*Independent*, 15 November 1996). These are opportunities which are open to us because of privatization and liberalization and we are seizing them.

If software is going to be crucial to economic reforms in the next century, the other factor will be access to financial capital in a world where there are a host of investment opportunities clamouring for finance. Our well-developed capital markets, so criticized by the Labour Party for their supposed short-termism, are actually a very effective vehicle for putting investment into new technology. Biotechnology for example is an extraordinarily exciting industry for the future. Germany has virtually no significant biotechnology companies because of a combination of heavy-handed regulation and the inability of new firms to raise finance. By contrast, the City of London has enabled many new biotechnology start-ups to raise the capital they need. Indeed, one of the firms newly in Britain's largest companies is a biotechnology firm which as yet has no product, merely a research team with some patents.

The pressures from capital markets ensure that every pound invested is put to work much harder in Britain than on the Continent. Their opaque accountancy rules and the absence of takeover threat mean that capital is not set to work efficiently. Companies can trundle on for years without earning a proper return on the money which has been invested into them and is supposed to pay the pensions and the insurance claims of the future.

We are also well placed to seize an economic advantage from our public-sector reforms. Attending an OECD conference on public-sector reform last year, it was clear that our main competitors now wanted to learn from us about privatizing, deregulating and creating markets within the public sector. This was driven by a hard-headed recognition that if you can hold down the cost of your public sector and ensure that it delivers high-quality services without imposing an excessive tax burden then that gives your economy a crucial competitive advantage. The fact that our energy prices are much lower than those on the Continent, that our health service costs much less than health care in America, and that our railway system is now enjoying a revival after privatization, all give a new edge to Britain's competitive advantage.

The critics claim 'globalization' means a world where commercial activity shifts around restlessly in pursuit of the cheapest labour. But it is not quite as simple as this. Why is so much of the world's foreign-exchange dealing done in the City of London? Why are most of the world's motor-racing cars designed and maintained within fifty miles of Oxford? The explanations for this clustering are complex but they include tough domestic competition, informed consumers and mobile individuals taking expertise from company to company. We have been called 'The Silicon Valley of motor sport' because 'Intense rivalry exists at all levels of the competitive car industry from teams to components. Companies spin off from each other and individuals move from employer to employer in a high-pressure process that fosters rapid innovation as well as continuous information flow and exchange' (Professor Porter, *The Competitive Advantage of Nations*, 'Summary', p. 11). It is a world away from that stale agenda of grants, handouts, tax breaks, new regulations on corporate governance, the Social Chapter, and the minimum wage, which constitute so-called New Labour's industrial strategy. These clusters have rarely emerged as a result of state action but they do have strong cultural roots and they survive, indeed thrive, in an open, competitive environment where individualism reigns and small business can thrive. It is significant that only 5 per cent of British small firms cite domestic laws and taxes as a constraint on their expansion compared with a European average of over 30 per cent.

Our massive success in attracting firms from abroad shows that we are the world's favourite economy. At the very same time as our left-wing politicians make the pilgrimage to Brussels to pay homage to the Continental system, so the businessmen from those countries are desperately shifting their investments, factories, and jobs over here.

Opportunity For All

The ultimate arguments for this type of open competitive economy are not economic at all. They are moral and social. They give individuals the greatest scope for taking control over their own lives and they create a society which is inclusive and meritocratic. This is why we call the political programme to deliver this vision, 'Opportunity For All'.

The crucial distinction between the two main parties is whether we are to have the opportunity of making our own way in the world or whether instead the overall objective is to make us more equal. It is striking that even when Labour wish to support meritocratic policies they do so on the grounds that

103

it will make us all equal and create greater 'social cohesion' even when there is no evidence that it would. Indeed it is one of the paradoxes that those who make the most rhetorical play with the politics of inclusion advocate at the same time policies whose practical effects are exclusion. Britain and America are much more open and mobile societies than the heavily regulated ones of the Continent.

There are still many on the Left who have a picture of Britain as a country divided by snobbery and class barriers. Yet the latest list of the richest 500 people in the country assembled by the *Sunday Times* showed a rapid decline in the proportion who had inherited their wealth and no fewer than six who were sons of miners. One recent study suggested half of all adult men in Britain are in a different class from the one their fathers were in at the same age – a higher level of social mobility than just about any other advanced Western country.

The most important single factor in driving people up or down the social scale is ability. The National Child Development Study has been tracking all the children born in the first week of March 1958. It shows that the children born to a disadvantaged background were overwhelmingly likely to move up the earnings scale provided they simply obtained some qualification. If they got as far as an A level or a higher-level qualification they were seven times more likely to move up the social scale than to stay where they were. Indeed, Peter Saunders has shown in a fascinating paper for the Institute for Economic Affairs that scores in simple general-ability tests taken when a child was seven were a much stronger predictor of the social class of that child twenty-two years later than was the class of the parents at the time they sat the test.

Raising educational standards and spreading educational opportunities are therefore crucial Conservative tasks for the fifth term. Children are so diverse that the best way to serve them all is to allow schools to be diverse too, and that is why we are going to allow schools to select more pupils by aptitude or ability. Schools can only work well if they are calm and orderly places and if the teachers are clear that they are transmitting values and a canon of knowledge which stands above the relativism that says nothing is worth anything more than anything else. Labour, by contrast, have made a mess of schooling in the areas which they control through LEAs. They want to take child benefit away from children who stay on at school to study for A levels and to get rid of the Assisted Places Scheme, which is so successful in enabling children from modest backgrounds to move up the educational ladder. Tony Blair made it clear at his party conference in 1996 that he is still committed to traditional comprehensives, which are often no better than the secondary moderns whose failure brought down the previous eleven-plus system.

Opportunity for all also means getting people off welfare and into work and, as we saw in Chapter 5, here too there is an ambitious Conservative agenda of ensuring that people are better off in work than out of work. At the same time we are delivering the support and encouragement to help those who may have given up hope back into work. These measures also identify fraudulent claims by people who are working in the black economy.

There is another way in which we Conservatives believe in spreading opportunity for all – people should have the opportunity to acquire the savings and the insurance cover which will mean they need not be dependent on the state in times of adversity. One of the historic strengths of our country has been that we had a mass of social provision long before the state muscled in on the act. As Benjamin Franklin observed when he visited the country in 1766, 'There is no country in the world where so many provisions are established for them [the poor]; so many hospitals to receive them when they are sick and lame, founded and maintained by voluntary charities; so many alms houses for the aged of both sexes . . .' It is not just a matter of charity any more; there is also massive scope for personal saving and commercial insurance. After all, we now are sufficiently prosperous to be able to put some money aside for a rainy day. Again, one of Britain's great strengths is that we have one of the world's most sophisticated financial services industries. It has already shown great skill in developing new products enabling us to save and insure against the vagaries of life and we must encourage this process still further. Britain owns over half of all of Europe's pensions savings.

As Peter Lilley has said:

Private provision of social security is already very extensive. For example, £52 billion a year of new investment in pension funds are made available to industry. Sixty per cent of the working population are covered by employers' sickness schemes. And 15 million households have some form of life assurance. 1.3 million people have permanent health insurance policies. About one million homeowners, and over a quarter of those taking out new mortgages, insure their mortgages. Friendly societies still have some 16 million members and pay out some £600 million a year. On top of this about three-quarters of those eligible to opt out of the State Earnings Related Pension scheme do so. Beveridge always wanted to see private provision supplement and complement state welfare. We are determined to carry this vision further, and rein in the growth of public expenditure in ways which encourage greater private provision. (*Winning the Welfare Debate*, Social Market Foundation, 1995, p. 45)

If we can spread opportunity by an open labour market, high-quality education, helping people off welfare into work, and encouraging private savings, then we will deliver the Tory vision of an inclusive, property-owning democracy. The stakeholder economies of the Continent are all about protecting organized groups recognized by the state against individuals who dare to be different. They favour insiders over outsiders. Our agenda tears down such barriers and spreads opportunity much more widely.

The Progressive Attack on the Hard-Working Classes

So far we have looked at a future of enterprise and opportunity. But we need a still point in a changing world. That must come from values which are widely shared amongst the British people and which they expect public institutions ranging from schools and the benefits system through to the BBC to transmit and sustain. They are the values of what have been called the hard-working classes. Opposed to them is the modern liberal progressive who tolerates an extraordinary variety of opinion, of lifestyle and behaviour, while at the same time he does not see any reason for variations in personal affluence because property inheritance and reward have little meaning for him. It is the typical world view of the twentieth-century progressive: diversity in everything apart from income and wealth, where egalitarianism reigns.

The sort of people we Conservatives have in mind when we formulate our policies for the future are the couple, perhaps living on a modest income, struggling to bring up their children decently and trying to make a better life for their families. Often they feel that their efforts are mocked. They are mocked if the benefits system and housing policies seem to give an almost similar income and accommodation to people who are not hard at work earning the money to pay for it. They are mocked if the local school fails to stand up for the types of behaviour which they are trying to instil at home. They feel that they are battling against a hostile environment if the TV and the radio are promulgating a shallow and cynical view of the world. For much of the twentieth century clever people have been thinking of evermore ingenious arguments which in the long run undermine these values. What Conservatives want to do through schools and taxes and benefits and improvements in public order is to make it clear that we are on the side of those decent people and their much-mocked principles. This has always been the traditional strength of British Conservatism. Disraeli observed:

If it does not represent national feeling, Toryism is nothing. It does not depend upon hereditary coteries of exclusive nobles. It does not attempt power by attracting to itself the spurious forces which may accidentally arise from advocating cosmopolitan principles or talking cosmopolitan jargon.

Values are embodied in and transmitted by institutions – and we weaken them at our peril. That is why we are so opposed to those left-wing progressives who appear to regret that unlike other European nations, we have not had the inestimable advantage of military defeat or revolution to wipe the slate clean and start again. Labour want to modernize us by remaking us as a Continental democracy *circa* 1980 and they have found a powerful new instrument to do it: European federalism. Indeed, by abandoning the veto in many areas, they will be giving other countries the power to reshape us and our institutions, whatever the objections of the British Government.

De Gaulle was supposed to have 'une certain idée de la France'. Conservatives have a certain idea of Great Britain. The individual, enterprise, and commerce are at the heart of it. So is something else: recognition that we are endowed as richly with institutions as any other country in the world. Those institutions – some public and national, many private and local – have emerged over centuries of limited government and have been threatened this century, as never before, by the rise of big government. They shape our behaviour and give our country its stability. It is why Conservative patriotism is not quite the same as the blood and soil nationalism of the Continental variety. We love our country because we love its institutions and the way of life they sustain.